St John of Bridlington
His Life and Legacy

The last Englishman
to be made a saint before the
Reformation

John Wardle

St John of Bridlington – His Life and Legacy

© John Wardle – March 2013

ISBN: 978-0-9535862-6-4

Published by John E. Eckersley

Cartographic and artistic presentation by Mark Comer

Printed by The Max Design & Print Co, Dunnington, York

Front cover picture: Prior John and the Hartlepool sailors
from *'A Burlington Tale'* by Sharon Winter

Rear cover picture: The window, installed in the south aisle of the Priory in 1949, showing Robert the Scribe, St John of Bridlington and George Ripley the Alchemist

The author is most grateful to the Lords Feoffees and Assistants of the Manor of Bridlington for generously sponsoring the publication of this book.

St John of Bridlington - His Life and Legacy

Contents

	List of illustrations	4
	Foreword by the Bishop of Hull	5
	Acknowledgements	6
	Preface	7
Chapter 1	The Early Life of the Augustinian Community	9
Chapter 2	The Life of John de Thweng	19
Chapter 3	The Path to Canonisation	29
Chapter 4	Pilgrimage and Popularity	37
Chapter 5	The Legacy of St John	51
	Notes	55
	Glossary of terms	57
Appendix A	The Middle English Verse Life of Prior John	58
Appendix B	Sources and select bibliography	63
Appendix C	Last Wills and Testaments	67
Appendix D	Grants and Charters	68
Appendix E	Miracles attributed to Prior John de Thweng	69
Appendix F	Other medieval documents	70
Appendix G	A comparative date chart	71
Appendix H	Liturgical resources	72

*This book is dedicated to the memory of Richard Dooks,
Bridlington Priory churchwarden, 1996-2002*

List of Illustrations

Front cover	A painting of Prior John and the Hartlepool sailors	*(Sharon Winter)*
	A section of cloister arcading from 'A Reconstruction of Bridlington Priory'	*(John Earnshaw)*
Back cover	The Priory's St John window (with Robert the Scribe and George Ripley, Alchemist)	*(John Wardle)*
Chapter 1	A conjectural reconstruction of the Priory church and buildings	*(Les Turner)*
	The Monastic Opus Dei	*(Mark Comer)*
	Plan of the monastic buildings	*(John Earnshaw)*
	The churches and lands of Bridlington Priory	*(Bernard Jennings)*
	Houses of monks and canons in Yorkshire by the early 13th century	*(Bernard Jennings)*
Chapter 2	The Norman font in All Saints' Church, Thwing	*(John Wardle)*
	An Augustinian canon in full habit	*(Marmaduke Prickett)*
	All Saints' Church, Thwing	*(John Wardle)*
	St John window, Bridlington Priory	*(John Wardle)*
	St John window, All Saints' Church, Thwing	*(John Wardle)*
Chapter 3	A page from the 1401 Bull of Canonisation	*(Archivium Segretum Vaticanum)*
	A conjectural reconstruction of the shrine of St John	*(John Earnshaw)*
	An inscribed picture of a sailing ship from the shrine	*(John Walker)*
	A conjectural restoration of the shrine by J.S. Purvis	*(John Walker)*
	A page from the Calendar, Bridlington Breviary	*(John Wardle)*
Chapter 4	Henry V on the Hyperion CD insert	*(Hyperion Records)*
	Pilgrim badges	*(Museum of London)*
	The window in Morley Church showing St John and St William of York	*(John Wardle)*
	St John in a window of the Beauchamp Chapel, Warwick	*(John Wardle)*
	A miniature of St John in the Beaufort Hours	*(© The British Library Board, Royal 2 A. XVIII, f.7v)*
	The Wollaton Antiphonal cantus firmus 'Quem malignus spiritu'	*(Manuscripts & Special Collections, The University of Nottingham)*
	The Priory seal attached to the 1445 relics certificate	*(Eton College)*
	The St John window in Ludlow Parish Church	*(John Wardle)*
	A screen painting of St John in the Church at Hempstead-by-Eccles	*(John Wardle)*
	Map showing places connected with St John of Bridlington	*(Mark Comer)*
Chapter 5	The Bayle gatehouse today	*(John Wardle)*
	The Priory Choristers celebrating their RSCM awards in 2011	*(Simon Kench)*
	The Priory West End today	*(Simon Kench)*

Foreword by the Bishop of Hull

"There was a man sent from God, whose name was John."

Those words were originally about John the Baptist, but could be applied to St John of Bridlington... ...or John Wardle.

As plans are made to celebrate the 900th birthday of Bridlington Priory, it is timely to reflect on its history and in particular on the life of its remarkable 14th century Prior, John of Bridlington.

His name is on several street signs in Bridlington, and indeed there is a popular pub called The Prior John, but few people know much about him.

In this book, John Wardle has sought to address this lack of knowledge. In his accessible, well researched and perceptive writing, he has succeeded in communicating not only the basic facts of the history of the Priory in general and St John of Bridlington in particular, but also something of St John's legacy and contemporary relevance.

The life of a 14th century Augustinian monk is almost unimaginable today; stories surrounding St John of Bridlington make it hard always to separate fact from legend; the world has changed beyond recognition. Nevertheless, what John Wardle calls "the three great monastic themes" are still relevant today.

Prayer, study and hospitality: all three still feature prominently in the life of Bridlington Priory. John Wardle, himself Rector of the Priory at the start of the 21st century, is well placed to make the connections between then and now. My hope is that this publication will be an encouragement to many to make those same links.

Richard Frith,
Bishop of Hull

Acknowledgements

The author would like to thank the following for permission to reproduce material in this book:

Sharon Winter, for the front cover picture, part of her larger work 'A Burlington Tale', and Bridlington Old Town Association, owners of the painting.

Prof. Bernard Jennings, for the maps in Chapter 1 and information about the early life of the Priory.

Dr Juliana Dresvina for the information about the connection between St John of Bridlington and St John of Beverley, and the details of many medieval manuscripts.

The Lords Feoffees and Assistants of the Manor of Bridlington, for the Priory conjectural reconstruction and the image of the calendar in the Bridlington Breviary.

Dr Anna Howard (née Parsons) for an index of the contents of the Bridlington Breviary.

Mr Gerald Moxon and Dr Rob Lutton, for translations of the medieval Latin sources.

The editorial team of Neuphilologische Mitteilungen, Helsinki for the Middle English Verse Life.

Mrs Nicky Terry, for the translation of the Middle English Verse Life of St John.

Mr Philip Weller, for his notes for the CD, 'Music for Henry V and the House of Lancaster'.

Hyperion Records for the image from the front cover of their CD 'Music for Henry V and the House of Lancaster'.

The Vatican Secret Archives, for the image of a page from the 1401 Bull of Canonisation.

The British Library, for the image of St John from Manuscript Royal 2A.

Manuscripts and Special Collections, The University of Nottingham for the image of the 'Quem malignus spiritu' plainsong in the Wollaton Antiphonal.

The Museum of London for the images of the pilgrim badges.

Eton College, Windsor, for the image of the 1445 certificate.

Dr Roger Bowers, for material from his U.E.A. PhD thesis on Choral Institutions.

Mr John Walker, for the drawing of the shrine by J.S. Purvis and various photographs of the woodwork in St Oswald's Church, Flamborough.

Mr Simon Kench, photographer, for the photographs of the Priory choristers.

Dr A.I. Doyle and the staff of Durham University Library and the Durham Cathedral Chapter Library.

The incumbents of the parish churches of Ludlow, Morley, Thwing and Warwick for the stained glass window images; the incumbent of Hempstead-by-Eccles for the screen painting image.

Preface

I remember very clearly when I first heard about St John of Bridlington. It was shortly after my arrival as Rector of the Priory Church of St Mary in Bridlington in March 1999. The late Richard Dooks, churchwarden, started to give me a short history lesson about his native town and very soon mentioned the saint – Bridlington's most famous person. Richard was always enthusiastic about the Priory and whetted my appetite to find out more about its special prior and saint. I soon realised that John de Thweng was the last Englishman to be canonised before the Reformation – what a claim to fame!

Over the ensuing years I preached several sermons on or around the 10th October, St John's feast day. I heard from those who had attended the celebration at Thwing in 1979 which marked the 600th anniversary of John's death. In 2001 the Priory celebrated the 600th anniversary of his canonisation by Pope Boniface IX; the preacher on that occasion was the Revd Fr Michael Loughlin, the local Roman Catholic priest. History was made then; that must have been the first such sermon in the Priory since the Reformation!

In March 2003, a Russian student called Juliana Dresvina called at the Rectory and asked to look round the Priory. I took her and her companion into church and as we walked round I pointed out the window in the south aisle depicting St John and discovered that she had come from Oxford in search of St John. She kindly sent me her academic paper which deals with the blurring of the cults of the two saints, John of Beverley and John of Bridlington. Juliana's visit encouraged my interest in St John, and I was to find her researches invaluable, especially in locating sources and manuscripts.

The Bishop of Hull agreed to my request for a three month sabbatical in 2005 and I decided to find out more about St John, with a view to writing his life story. There is very little about him in print which is generally accessible, just the usual paragraphs in guide books and the like, and rather mysterious references to medieval Latin manuscripts in famous libraries.

I was fortunate in being able to visit the British Library, Durham Cathedral Chapter and University Libraries, and several churches in the Midlands with windows depicting St John. However, the climax to my travels was a visit to the Secret Vatican Archives in Rome where I saw for myself the document of canonisation from 1401 in which John, Prior of Bridlington, was declared a saint and confessor.

I am most grateful for the financial support I received for my sabbatical researches from the Ecclesiastical Insurance Group and the Diocese of York.

During 2005, several friends drew my attention to material which was available locally, in both public and private libraries. I am grateful to David Burnett, the late Philip Cawthorne, Michael Chaddock, Sarah Hutchinson (née Stocks), Sue Reeves, Delia Smith and John Walker, amongst others, for their help.

As the story of John de Thweng was originally written in medieval Latin, I needed some help with the translation of the sources. I am very grateful to the late Gerald Moxon, a retired classics teacher and a member of the church of Our Lady and

St Peter in Bridlington, for the many hours he spent translating the Latin, and for his interest in this project. After the death of Gerald, the Latin translations were finished by Dr Rob Lutton of Nottingham University, to whom I am most grateful.

I am indebted greatly to Canon Purvis, a Bridlington man and York historian, who wrote a booklet about St John in 1924. He was a true scholar and based his material on the earliest sources of the saint's life. I have used Canon Purvis' translation of the 1401 Papal Bull and his notes on the miracle stories and stained glass windows connected with St John.

An independent 'picture' of St John is found in some Middle English verses, probably written in 1379 by a minstrel who knew the Priory and its Prior well. We know that John enjoyed the regular visits of minstrels. I am very grateful to Dr Ian Doyle of Durham University for providing me with a copy of the poem and to Nicky Terry, a retired Bridlington English teacher, for a translation of the verses into modern English.

I was delighted when a new CD was released by Hyperion in August, 2011. Called 'Music for Henry V and the House of Lancaster', it is based on the Office of St John found in the Wollaton Antiphonal and includes the anonymous three-part Mass setting in honour of St John. I am indebted to Philip Weller of the Music Department at Nottingham University for his help in exploring this valuable resource.

I would like to thank those who read the proofs and made helpful suggestions:
- Michael Chaddock
- John Eckersley
- Anthony Halford
- Helen Hughes
- David Mooney
- Robin Sharpe
- Linda Wardle
- William Wardle
- Canon David Weston

I also received encouragement from Prof. Bernard Jennings, who kindly allowed me to use material from his book, *Yorkshire Monasteries*. Last, but not least, my sincere thanks to my publisher, John Eckersley, Mark Comer for the design and layout, Carrie Geddes my distributor and the Lords Feoffees for their advice, expertise and support.

I have tried throughout to provide a readable account of St John's life, and to avoid cluttering the text with countless references. However, there is much material in both Latin and English which needs noting and documenting. This will be available in print and in electronic form for anyone who would like to take the matter further.

A glossary of terms is included to help with the language of the monastic life.

John Wardle.
The Feast of St John of Bridlington,
10 October, 2012

Chapter 1

The Early Life of the Augustinian Community

In writing of St John of Bridlington, John de Thweng, we must first consider the early life of the community of which he became the Prior.

By the 12th century, Yorkshire had a number of religious communities of various kinds. Bridlington Priory was founded in about 1113 as an Augustinian house, and was one of the first of its kind in the north of England. Hexham Abbey was established as an Augustinian Priory in the same year.

The Augustinian order had been introduced into England with the founding of St Botulph's Priory at Colchester in about 1095. Augustinian canons were priests who lived in communities, holding everything in common, and living according to the Rule of St Augustine. He was Bishop of Hippo in North Africa until his death in 430 AD. When he became a bishop and had to leave the monastic community he had founded, he wrote a list of rules for the members to follow in his absence.[1] His general advice was to have all things in common, to pray together at appointed times, to dress without distinction and to obey a superior. The Rule, as it became known, was a later compilation composed of Augustine's original precepts combined with parts of his sermons and commentaries. Its strength was its flexibility, being adaptable to geography and circumstances, compared to the much more prescriptive Rule of St Benedict.[2]

The foundation of these priories, as they were called in Yorkshire, was encouraged by popes and bishops, and in England by King Henry I (1100-35). The new priory at Bridlington was founded by Walter de Gant, with the blessing of Archbishop Thurstan. We read in the founding charter: 'I, Walter de Gant, notify to all sons of Holy Church that I have established Canons Regular in the Church of St Mary of Bridelington by the desire and assent of King Henry, for his soul, and for the souls of my father and mother, my own, and my friends. I therefore grant to the same Church and those serving there whatever I had in the same vill, namely thirteen carucates of land with the mills adjoining'.[3] It was initially given an endowment of five parish churches, rising eventually to eighteen.

Walter de Gant's father, Gilbert, was a powerful Norman baron, originally from Ghent in Flanders, who had come to England in 1066 with William, Duke of

Normandy. He helped suppress the risings in the north and was granted large estates by William; his principal Yorkshire manor was at Hunmanby.

It is interesting to note that the 11th century parish of Bridlington included nine other townships in addition to Bridlington itself – Bempton, Buckton, Easton, Grindale, Hilderthorpe, Marton, Sewerby, Speeton, Wilsthorpe together with part of Auburn.[4]

The basic complement of a priory was a prior and twelve canons, but the better endowed establishments often had larger numbers, perhaps twenty or more canons. For each canon the community needed an annual income of about £3, considerably less than the equivalent Benedictine monk required. The reason for this difference was that the canons were usually based in places where they could make the most of the support of the local parishes, with much of their endowment coming from the income of those parish churches. From the point of view of prospective benefactors, founding an Augustinian house was an attractive proposition – to use a modern phrase, it provided 'good value for money'.

Monks and Monasteries

It is too easy to call all members of religious communities 'monks', and to talk in general terms about the 'monasteries' of England. However, we need to distinguish between friars, monks and canons, as follows:

- **Friars** – the best-known were, and still are, Franciscan. Their main function was preaching; friars joined an order, not a house, and were expected to be much more mobile than monks or canons.
- **Monks** – belonged to a community which provided their 'spiritual home' and usually they had no responsibility outside its walls. Benedictines are the most famous example. Many were priests, others lay brothers.
- **Canons** – priests living under a rule (*regula* in Latin) and so known as 'regular canons' to distinguish them from the 'secular canons' who were part of cathedral or minster teams. They carried out their priestly duties, both sacramental and pastoral, in serving local parish churches.[5]

The difference between monks and canons has been described in terms of the famous New Testament sisters: monks were like Mary, the contemplative; canons were like Martha, the one who served (see chapter 4, 'Music in honour of St John', *Antiphons*). Whilst there is certainly some truth in that picture, it is too simplistic an analogy as both the Rules of Augustine and Benedict, for example, include worship and devotion alongside service to the local community, especially the care of the sick and infirm.

In the early years of the Priory at Bridlington, the small community there quickly started to build up its resources, in both churches and lands. By 1140 several donors, including the Percy family, had given eight more churches and much land. Henry I gave the Priory freedom from tolls, as well as authority over the manor of Bridlington. King Stephen re-affirmed these rights, and in addition gave the Priory control over the port of Bridlington. His charters included extra land containing over three-quarters of the township of Bridlington and more land in Hilderthorpe and Easton.

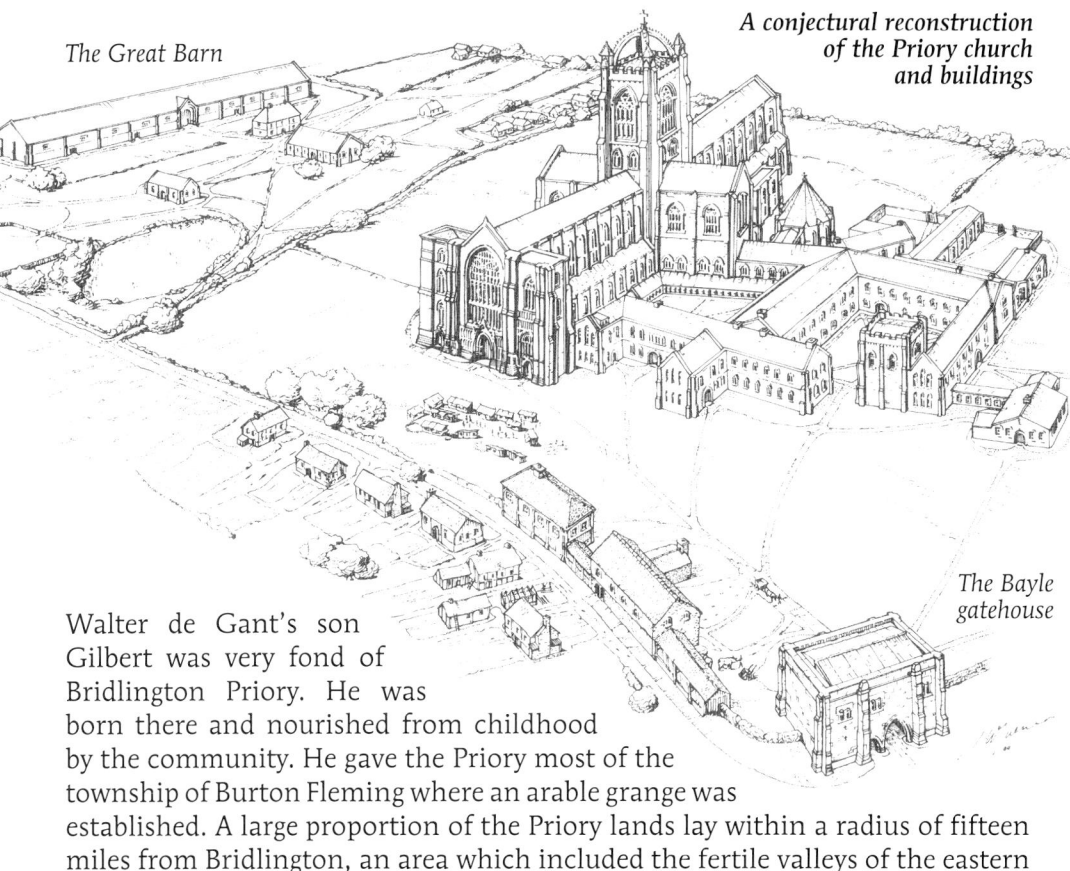

A conjectural reconstruction of the Priory church and buildings

The Great Barn

The Bayle gatehouse

Walter de Gant's son Gilbert was very fond of Bridlington Priory. He was born there and nourished from childhood by the community. He gave the Priory most of the township of Burton Fleming where an arable grange was established. A large proportion of the Priory lands lay within a radius of fifteen miles from Bridlington, an area which included the fertile valleys of the eastern Wolds, with their sheep and corn, and the heavier soils of northern Holderness. The principal sheep stations were on the edge of the high wolds, at Gristhorpe and Willerby.[6]

The Priory buildings were erected over a lengthy period of time in a rather piecemeal way, depending on the financial resources and manpower available. The first stone church, which would have been built in the Norman style, has left traces in the form of re-used masonry in the north aisle. Some of the earliest stone is to be found in the reconstructed cloister arcade of c. 1150-75. The north side of the nave dates from the early thirteenth century, with the south side being built later, from about 1260. By the time young John de Thweng entered the community in about 1340, the Priory church would have been large and magnificent and its ancillary buildings considerable in scope.

Prior Robert, 'the Scribe'

During its first hundred years, the Priory became established as a centre of learning. The leading figure was the fourth prior, Robert, known as 'the Scribe'. He wrote several commentaries on the Scriptures, three of which have survived.[7] The Priory had a busy *scriptorium*, where books were copied and illustrated. Robert listed in his *Dialogue (see later)* some of the work done there by the canons: preparing parchment for the scribes, writing books (i.e. copying), illuminating, ruling lines, writing musical notation, making corrections and binding books. Only a small number of books from the Priory library have survived; they include an illuminated copy of the Gospel according to St Mark in the British Library[8] and a breviary in the Bayle Museum in Bridlington.

Robert has left us a picture of community life at the Priory in his *Bridlington Dialogue,* written about 1150. It takes the form of an exchange between 'a master', Robert himself, and 'a disciple', a novice canon. It is a practical treatise, based on the Rule of St Augustine; from it, we can get a glimpse of a typical monastic day in Bridlington. The main ingredients were:

Worship (the 'divine office') The whole of the day was built around the life of prayer and community worship. The eight canonical ('regular') hours were:

- Matins at first light
- Prime (First hour) at dawn
- Terce (Third hour) at 9.00am
- Sext (Sixth hour) at noon.
- None (Ninth hour) at 3.00pm
- Vespers at sundown.
- Compline at 9.00pm
- Vigils at midnight.

Mass was celebrated daily, probably after Terce. Private prayer was encouraged and took place between the Hours; there was no set time nor rule to govern it. Prior Robert writes:

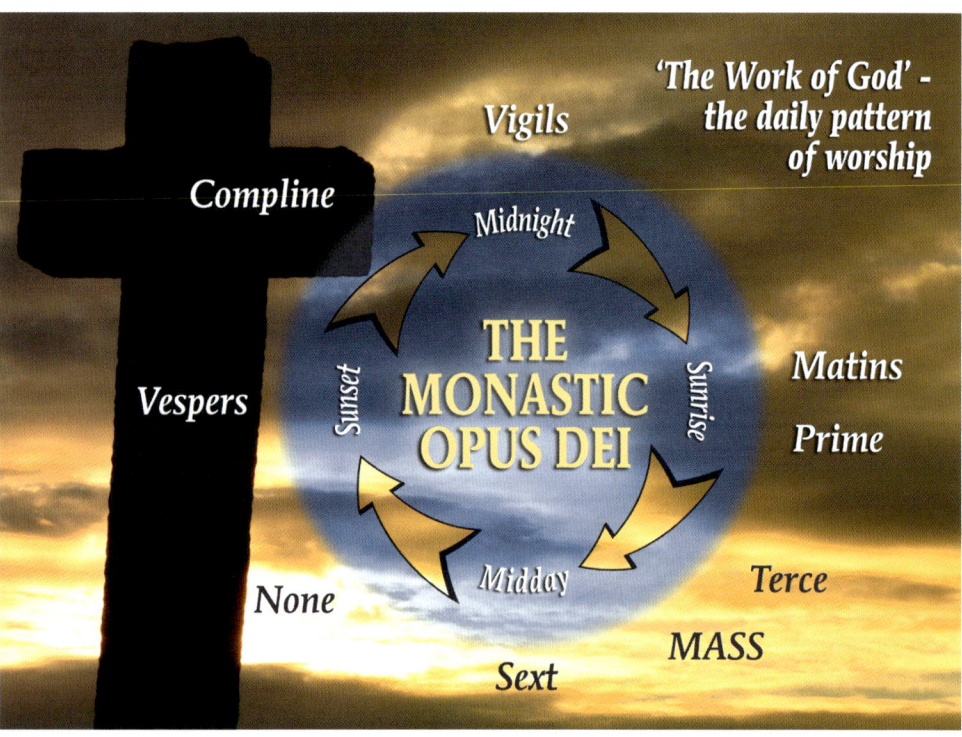

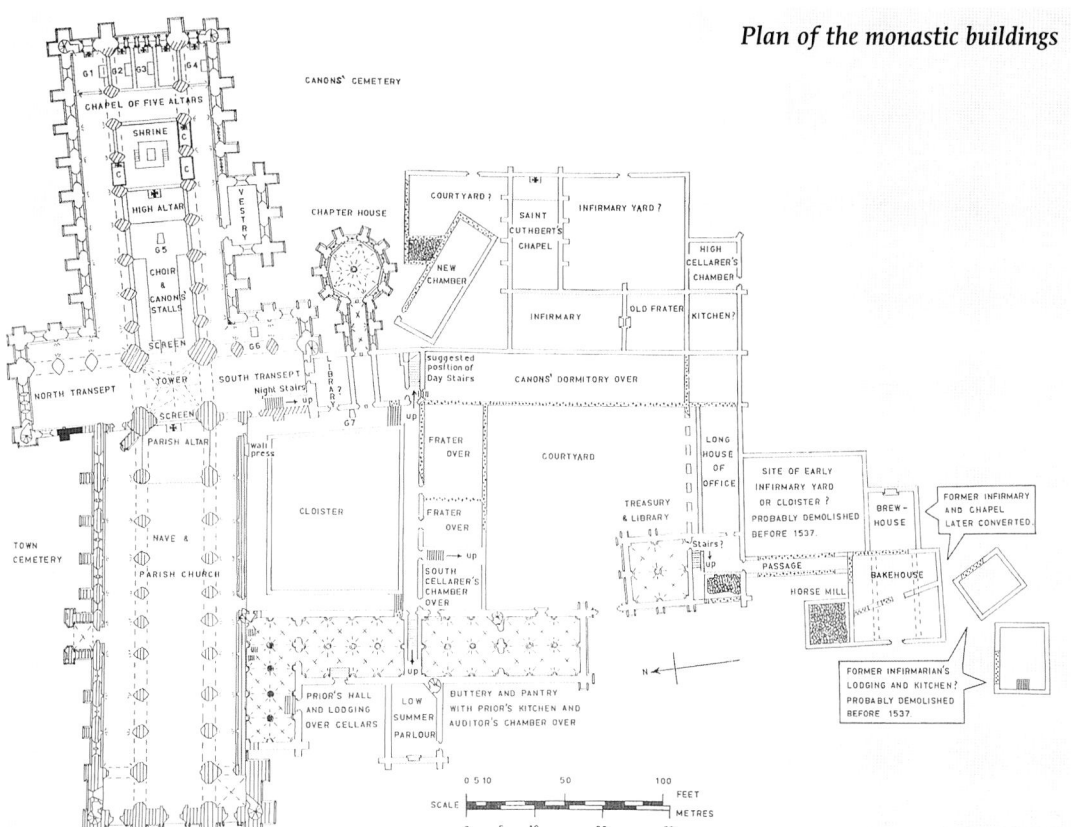

Plan of the monastic buildings

'It is a good and laudable thing to pour out private prayers to God, frequently and in purity of heart, in addition to these Canonical Hours which are ordained for us to say together, at least for those whose appointed tasks allow them some leisure to do so, and if their own free devotion prompts them to it. This must be done, however, not in a loud voice, but with profound attention of the heart and compunction of the mind, and with abundant tears; for we believe that God will listen to us if we pray like that. Hence the Lord says, *But thou, when thou prayest, enter into thy closet and, when thou hast shut the door, pray to thy Father in secret*'.[9]

After a detailed description of the eight 'hours' and their Biblical roots, Prior Robert comments:

'Such, then, is the catholic order of divine worship, which is kept immutably by the whole Church of Christ. But the fact that some people say Night Office and Matins together long before dawn, while others say them in broad daylight, though either course lacks reason, must perhaps be put down to the vice of drowsiness, compelling them by its own shameful sloth in the one case to celebrate divine service before the time and hour, and in the other after them. The former of these might well be compared, I think, to unripe grapes, the latter to rotten ones. So, in order that we ourselves may offer ripe and worthy grapes to God, it behoves us to keep strictly to the HOURS AND TIMES APPOINTED by our Rule for psalmody, and to be instant at the holy Offices, awaiting our life's end without anxiety, if it should find us occupied in such an act'.[10]

Chapter 1 / The early life of the Augustinian community

The churches and lands of Bridlington Priory

- Hayburn
- Scalby ✝
- ✝ Scarborough
- Gristhorpe
- Folkton
- Flotmanby
- ★ Filey
- Willerby ★● Staxton
- Muston
- ★ Ganton
- Hunmanby
- Fordon ●
- Reighton ●
- Speeton ●
- Wold Newton ●
- Buckton ●
- Burton Fleming
- Grindale ★
- ● Bempton
- Marton ●
- ✝ Flamborough
- Boynton ★
- Sewerby ●
- Rudston ●
- Bessingby ★
- ✤ BRIDLINGTON PRIORY
- Carnaby ★
- Haisthorpe ●
- Hilderthorpe ●
- Kilham ●
- Wilsthorpe ●
- Thornholme ●
- Auburn ●
- Fraisthorpe ●
- Nafferton ●
- Gransmoor ●
- Kelk ●
- Wansford ●
- Beeford ●
- Skirlington ●
- Hempholme ●
- Atwick ★
- Hornsea Burton ●
- Sproatley ✝
- Ottringham ✝

Scale: 1 – 3 – 5 miles

Legend:
- ★ Churches and Secular Estates
- ✝ Churches
- ● Other Secular Estates

Meals There were usually just two meals a day:
- Dinner (prandium), usually after Terce.
- Supper (cena), some time after None.

On fast days, those who were strong enough had supper only.

Sleep The canons retired after Compline, getting about two and a half hours sleep before they rose for Vigils; after that they would sleep until dawn.

Work The Superior apportioned the tasks, with much needing to be done for the common good. Examples were:
- Reading the Scriptures and expounding them to others.
- Practising singing or reading for the Offices.
- Working as scribes in the scriptorium, copying manuscripts.
- Making or mending clothes and shoes.
- Fashioning spoons, candlesticks, baskets, nets, rush mats, skeps (woven beehives).
- Kitchen work of all kinds.
- Outdoor work in the garden, tending vegetables, herbs and trees.
- Work in the fields, ploughing, seeding and harvesting.
- Keeping livestock, from sheep to bees.

The anonymous sister of the Community of St Mary the Virgin at Wantage, who translated the Dialogue into English, described life in the Priory community as follows:

'It is a pleasant picture of organised and unified activity, all done for God and for the common good, all very wholesome and English. The enclosure was strictly observed, only those whose business required it being allowed outside. Like all communities, this one at St Mary's, Bridlington, had its difficult members, and discipline was strict, but always loving and constructive in its aim. Those who were too old for work were cared for by the Infirmarian, and the sick came in for a specially tender, though never indulgent, attention.

The canons of Bridlington were surely fortunate in having Robert for their prior. He was a practical person, a typical common-sensical and forthright Yorkshireman. He was no mystic but was deeply spiritual, all the same. He never lost sight of love, the twin love of God and of one's neighbour, as the basic and ruling principle in all activities and all relationships'.[11]

At the beginning of the Dialogue, the Master quotes the Rule of St Augustine as his authority for the way in which the community of the Priory should be ordered, with its emphasis on the contributions of the individual members towards the common good and the harmony of the house. The eighteen sections of the Rule give as much detail about practical daily life, e.g. clothes and washing, as about the life of prayer and worship.

Some excerpts from the Bridlington Dialogue

The Dialogue, following the Rule, deals with nearly all aspects of community life. Before the detailed discussion gets under way, Robert uses a Biblical picture to describe the Priory's foundation:

Master: I happened on a certain little city… and the city's name was Bridlington. There at that time certain good sparrows, whose leader was the house of the heron and whose rock was plainly Christ, began to build their nests in the cedars of Lebanon which the Lord hath planted. The great and mighty cedars in this earthly Lebanon then were King Henry, Gilbert de Gant, Walter his son, and some others like them.[12]

In the section on prayer, the Novice is obviously concerned about the many hours spent at prayer in church:

OF PRAYER

Disciple: People often ask why we make such long prayers, and say not only a hundred psalms, but even a hundred and fifty over and over again in our prayers, when the Lord says in the Gospel, "But when ye pray, do not say much as do the heathen, thinking that they shall be heard for their much speaking".

Master: Although God knows everything before we ask of Him, we need prayer all the same, because the very attitude of prayer tranquillizes our heart, and cleanses it, and makes it roomier to receive the divine gifts that are poured upon us spiritually. In prayer, therefore, a turning of the heart takes place towards Him who is always ready to bestow the gift if we will take it.

Later on, the novice raises the matter of singing and reciting during worship:

OF SINGING

Disciple: What profit is there in singing, or in reading either, since it behoves us according to the Lord's injunctions always to pray, and not to cease there-from?

Master: You must know that the custom of singing in church was instituted not for spiritual persons, but for the carnal and imperfect, so that the sweetness of the chanting might melt the hearts of those whom the words left unmoved. For the flame of love and piety is kindled to a keener blaze when those same holy words are sung, than when they are not sung.

In the section of the Dialogue concerning 'Of Charity', the Novice asks his Master about the objects of love:

OF CHARITY

Disciple: I should like to know what are the 'all things', before which our Master bids that God be loved.

Master: Four things present themselves to every thoughtful person as objects of his love. First, that which is above us, that is, God. Second, that which we are ourselves. Third, that which is beside us, that is, our neighbour. Fourth, that which is below us, that is, our body.

There is a long section dealing with unity within the community and the holding of property:

OF COMMON PROPERTY

Master: A common life is a necessity for all, and supremely so for those who wish to serve beneath God's banner blamelessly. All men ought to have shared the use of all things in the world; but, because of iniquity, one calls this thing his own, another that.

Disciple: Go on now, and tell me what must be done with common property.

Master: This beyond doubt, which follows in the Rule, THAT THE SUPERIOR SHOULD DISTRIBUTE FOOD AND CLOTHING TO EVERY ONE OF YOU. ... TO THE SUPERIOR OBEDIENCE SHALL BE GIVEN AS TO A FATHER – that the superior should distribute to each not luxuries, but the things needful for life, lest maybe if each grabbed what and as much as he pleased, one indeed should hunger, while another got food.[13]

THE RULE OF ST AUGUSTINE

Augustinian tradition, following the advice of Augustine himself, was clear that the Rule should be read aloud weekly, and we can imagine that happening in the refectory or chapter house at Bridlington, not only in the time of Prior Robert, but also two hundred years later when John de Thweng became Prior. The Priory buildings were always in a state of flux, with change and re-building, but the spiritual foundation remained the same throughout the four centuries of the Priory's existence.

In the words of St Augustine,

'This Rule, held up before our mental eyes like a mirror, is bidden to be read to us once every week, so that our inward face may be beheld in it. There indeed, we can recognize our blemishes, and our beauties too. There we can gauge how much we are advancing, and also how far we fall short of our advancement. And it is called a Rule not without reason; for it suffers nothing of hurtful excess to approach or to be present in the man to whom it is united in a zealous bond, a binding zeal'.[14]

After the time of Robert the Scribe, the Bridlington community continued to be a centre of learning. Professor Jennings writes of this time: 'Of all the major orders of monks and canons, the Augustinians placed the highest value on scholarship. Bridlington stands well in this company... Two Bridlington canons of the fourteenth century were important literary figures. Peter of Langtoft wrote, in French and in verse, a history of the country from the ancient Britons to the death of Edward I in 1307. The name of the second author is unknown. He wrote a chronicle of the reign of Edward II (1307-27). One of his sources was a book in the Priory library, *Incidentia Chronicorum*'.[15]

Medieval Bridlington was not always a peaceful place. In the late 13th and early 14th centuries, England was at war with Scotland and the town was vulnerable to attack from land and sea. In the autumn of 1322 Robert the Bruce invaded England and his forces converged on Edward II and his army at Byland Abbey. Edward fled to Pickering and then to Bridlington Priory where he spent the night. The Priory valuables were sent into Lincolnshire for safe keeping.[16]

Materially, the Priory continued to prosper, wealth being created mainly through farming and tithes from its churches. Barley was the principal crop and the Priory was a leading wool producer. Wool was exported from the Quay as well as from Filey and Kingston-upon-Hull. The Great Barn to the north of the church was used to store the harvests from local estates; corn would be ground at the Priory's four windmills and two water mills. The right to hold a weekly market and an annual fair in August dates back to 1200, during the reign of King John.[17]

Houses of monks and canons in Yorkshire by the early 13th century

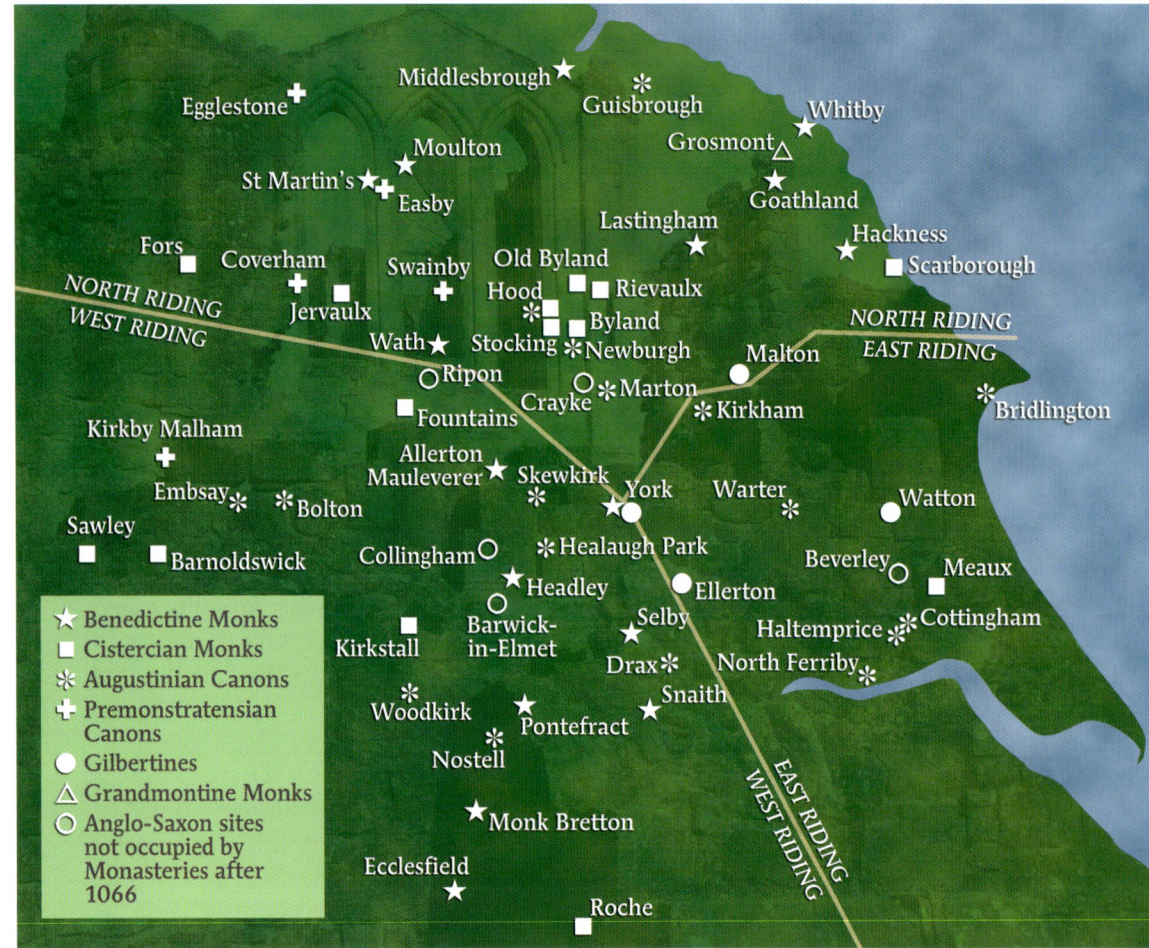

Chapter 2

The Life of John de Thweng

We find the details of John's life in five manuscripts:

1. The most important is that written by 'Canon Hugo' in about 1390, found in *Acta Sanctorum*. He was almost certainly a Bridlington canon, probably a contemporary of John de Thweng.
2. An incomplete Middle English Verse Life, probably written by a visiting minstrel around the time of John's death in 1379.
3. A biography in *Nova Legendae Angliae,* a collection made by Augustinian Friar John Capgrave from King's Lynn (died 1464).
4. A summary of John's life, written about 1530 by Bridlington Canon Thomas Ashby.
5. The Papal Bull of 1401.

Details of these, and all other sources, are given in Appendix B, Sources and select bibliography.

His early life

John was born in about 1320 in the village of Thwing in the Wolds, nine miles west of Bridlington. His parents were of some social standing, 'respectable Catholic Christian parents devoted to God in the kingdom of England ... and had honourable origins'.[1] The family name was probably *de Thweng*. This may have been a branch of the North Riding family of de Thweng which was settled at Kilton Castle near Loftus in Cleveland as early as 1257. They had estates at North Cave, Foxholes and Thwing. It is said that John was baptised in the church at Thwing, perhaps in the font which is still in use there today.

His earliest education was at his local village school from the age of five. The school would have been conducted by a priest or clerk, but not in the church, for Hugo writes: 'However, whenever he came out of school with his companions, and they as is their way applied themselves to childish sports and aimless dashing about, running this way and that, he himself would fly to the church. There on his own he gave himself up to prayer and devotion in a remarkable fashion at such a young age; as if taught by the grace of the Holy Spirit he utterly rejected all moral hazards and boyish habits, so that nowhere or only rarely there appeared in him any sign of boyish frivolity. A remarkable thing – who would ever be willing to believe it – that a five-year-old should abandon the activities and games of boyhood, and be given up to holiness and devotion'.[2]

He remained at the Thwing school for several years, taking a private vow of chastity at the age of twelve. He became a novice at the Priory when he was fourteen, but during the six years of his novitiate spent two years as a student at Oxford. 'While he was a student at Oxford, he frequently missed the searching debates into fallacies and dedicated the temple of his spirit to the supreme Lord. He was devoutly borne up by a warm passion for God and his neighbour, as indeed we have heard from the accounts of certain truthful fellow-students of his, at a young age heartily devoted to God, and against insults, threats and reproaches directed at himself he was gentle, peaceful and quiet.'[3]

The Norman font in the Church of All Saints, Thwing

After returning home he had a period as tutor to the children of a local worthy family, and finally entered the monastery at the age of twenty. 'On the Monday nearest before the feast of the martyr St Valentine (1340), John of Thweng received the canonical habit, as also did his companion, John of Snaith. And the following year on the Wednesday on which ashes are given, they were professed.'[4]

Right from the start, John's qualities were apparent. Hugo applies to him the Biblical text, "There was a man sent from God, whose name was John".[5]

John's duties as a Canon

It is possible to describe John's appearance as a professed canon of the Priory. Traditionally, Augustinian canons wore a black cassock for everyday duties. The complete habit also included a white rochet (a vestment resembling a surplice) worn over the cassock and a black cloak with hood to keep out the cold. A hat or biretta might also be worn outside. We can be almost certain that the Bridlington canons had beards. The remains of Prior Robert Brystwyk who died in 1493 were discovered in 1821 near the site of the south transept and his beard was intact.[6] The Middle English verse describes John as 'a handsome and attractive man, quiet and well mannered and full of goodness'.[7]

John rose rapidly through the ranks, becoming a priest and 'master of the novices and instructor of youths'.

Next he became the Cellarer and fulfilled the duties 'diligently, faithfully and discreetly'. These duties were wide-ranging, often taking him outside the monastery as he supervised the estates and the granges, paid attention to repairs of the buildings, allotted their tasks to the tillers of the fields and to other workers, regulated and provided bread, drink and other things according to the consumption of everyone, inside and outside the community. However, John did have his critics within the community who threatened to betray him to the Prior for giving too much food away to the poor, often secretly.

Hugo gives us the details of one such occasion when John seemed to be in trouble: 'It happened on another day at a time after this, when John the Cellarer himself wanted to go out, that the Prior was standing close to the path along which he was going to pass, together with some people who had accused him. Indeed, God's servant John himself, carefully thinking of the needy and the poor, brought some loaves with him, and carrying them secretly under his cape, was intent on carrying out his work of mercy and piety, as had been his custom before. The Prior, seeing him going out, then called him by name, saying: "John, come here". But he immediately obeyed the command of the Prior and came before him. The Prior asked him what he was carrying, and John, wishing his good works to be known only to God, as a simple and innocent person, bowed his head and replied to Father Prior. "Father," he said, "they are stones which I want to take out to improve the road outside the gate," meaning by an honest excuse of this sort to cover up wisely the works of his pious purpose, not because of his Prior, who was aware of his holy secrets, but because of the others who were standing there with the Prior. Then the Prior said to him, "Show us, my son, so that we may see if they are truly stones". He straight away obeying the command of his superior openly showed them the loaves he was carrying, which in their eyes seemed to be stones. The Prior certainly was amazed at this, gave him permission to go away, and said to those who were standing with him, "See what a silly charge you have brought to me against this kind, humble and innocent person". They indeed were surprised and struck with great shame, and returned to the cloister taking their folly with them. Later on they abandoned the malice of their wrong-headedness, and always held John himself in love and reverence'.[8]

An Augustinian canon in full habit

Chapter 2 / The life of John de Thweng

All Saints' Church, Thwing

After some time as Cellarer, John became sub-Prior. When Prior Peter Appleby resigned in 1356, John was chosen by chapter to succeed him. However, John declined the invitation. Canon Peter de Cotes became prior, but on his death in 1362 John was unanimously elected to that post by the chapter of canons. This time the outcome was different:

'When the Prior of the same monastery died later on, all the canons assembled in the chapter house elected him as their Father and Prior, no doubt having first called on the Holy Spirit. They elected him at the age of thirty-seven, with unanimous agreement and assent, with no one at all objecting or contradicting. Some because of his holiness and devoutness, some because of his foresight in spiritual and temporal affairs, but all cried with one voice that worthy as he was of themselves and their monastery he was a most suitable Father and Governor.

As was always his custom, he addressed them in a kindly spirit, said that he was quite unworthy to undertake such a rank and such a burden, and for some time he held out and refused to agree. But as all the canons with one accord persisted in the same opinion about their choice, he himself feeling that the will of God was close to him in this matter, encouraged by the advice of certain wise persons, and at the same time overcome by all the prayers, although reluctant, he was at last compelled by some means or other to give his agreement to his election.

He was also presented to the Archbishop of York, and according to the rites of the country, he was lawfully confirmed by the same Archbishop as perpetual Prior of the same monastery'.[9]

John the Prior

Canon Hugo describes life under John's leadership:

'By his holy merits and prayers the affairs and business of the monastery both in spiritual as in temporal matters remained in a good state throughout the period that he was Prior. Night and day in the cloister, in the choir and elsewhere he kept to the observance of the rule, just as when he was younger. Rarely indeed was he absent from reciting the canonical hours in choir, unless because of guests and other people who had arrived, or when a more serious reason concerning the business of the monastery was pressing on him; and he himself lived amongst his brothers like one of them. He always loved the straight way, and kept to the middle from both sides, not veering to the right by exalting himself for his rank and his merits, nor to the left, by giving in to partiality and the faults of human frailty.

Although he had a fine and spacious chamber, with certainly all its furnishings and decorations, that had been allotted from days long past to the holder of the office of Prior, in which the other Priors his predecessors had been accustomed to sit and to rest at night, John on the other hand, thinking this vanity, refused to sleep in the chamber itself, but every night he rested in one cell with the community in the common dormitory. His bedding and his clothing were of very little value, but rather cheap and coarse, yet decent and befitting his religious profession'.[10]

Capgrave adds that John used lambskins, the dress of the poor, rather than furs to keep himself warm in what was so often a cold monastery.[11]

John at worship

The monastic day was built upon a framework of worship, the *Opus Dei*. There were eight offices spread throughout the day and a daily celebration of Mass *(see Chapter 1)*. The Prior was expected to set an example to his fellows by his attendance at worship. John went 'the extra mile'.

'On whatever night John used to rise with the others also for the office of Matins, and frequently before the others, and devoted some time in the choir to devout prayers and holy meditations. When the office of Matins was over, he sometimes returned with the community to the dormitory, and going into his cell he would pretend that like the others he was going back to sleep in his own place, but afterwards when he perceived that his other brothers were sleeping, he would return from the dormitory to the church unnoticed; sometimes either there or in the chapter-house or other dedicated place he spent the rest of the day right until dawn in contemplation, psalms and other devout prayers, and so in general he continued serving God throughout his holy and religious life.'[12]

Prior John really did seem to 'burn the candle at both ends of the day', as Canon Hugo relates:

'When Compline was over, he was in the habit of staying behind alone in the choir. There with the greatest devotion he gave some time to prayer and contemplation, going over within himself and considering the state of his life, the care of souls and the governance of the monastery entrusted to him, also what he had done in his daily actions, if perhaps he had offended God by some negligence, knowing that as a mortal man he would give account of all these things. From that hour until the morning of the next day he would not speak with anyone, unless because of the greatest need, or when another very pressing reason existed'.[13] (The community observed 'The Great Silence' from Compline until Matins.)

Of his sincerity and devotion during worship there can be no doubt. Canon Thomas Ashby writes: 'He also was accustomed to celebrate his Mass in the community at the dawn of the day with such great devotion and trembling, that often when he was reading the canon, drops of water fell in streams from his head and eyes, and it happened very frequently that because of his fear of the venerable sacrament he had to be held up by the support of a brother, in case he might fall'.[14]

In a similar vein are some words from the Middle English author:
'Also he loved often to pray on his own and many times he was caught up in a trance' ('vanysshed in his sprite').[15]

Caring for the poor

John always had a heart for the poor. He remitted the rents of poor tenants, maintained poor scholars out of the wealth of the monastery, and fed and clothed the poor. The compassion he showed as Cellarer never left him and became the theme of his time as Prior.

The Priory's St John window

'He was both liberal and generous in distributing food and drink – and in works of charity (alms) and that especially to the poor, for he would both feed and clothe them. Also he showed mercy to all who approached him in their need. He was a supreme source of help to all and cared for those from every walk of life.

He knew well how to comfort those in distress and cheer them, and he would care for those who were sick.'[16]

Hospitality at the Priory

John would sometimes visit the various churches and communities which depended on the Priory, and would also receive visiting officials and dignitaries in Bridlington. One such occasion is mentioned by Capgrave and the Papal Bull. An official of the Duke of Lancaster, 'who was a very harsh collector of taxes', was threatening 'irreparable damage to the monastery'. John was patient and tried to calm him down, at the same time warning him, "Look to it that by your vicious zeal for your master, which drives you daily to vex and seize our goods, you be not thrust down into Hell, there to pay the penalty for ever". In the morning the official returned, a changed man, vowing friendship to the monastery, which vow he steadfastly performed.[17]

The author of the Middle English life of St John describes the Prior at table:

'When entertaining frequent guests of varying rank, he was expert at making them feel at ease as they sat at table and, although he ate little himself, he always appeared happy and cheerful.

When he could, he engaged minstrels who played beautifully and he would listen to them devotedly as they helped him be aware of God. He was often generous to them with money or in kind, as they reported on their travels'.[18]

Some noblemen visited the Priory to see if what they had heard about John the Prior was true. They were received and dined in the appropriate manner, but although their host, the Prior, drank from a silver cup, as was the custom for noblemen, it contained only water. One of the visitors asked if he could taste from the Prior's cup, even though his own cup was full of wine. John, not wishing to reveal his secret abstinence, said a prayer over his cup and the nobleman, after tasting it, declared he had never tasted better wine![19]

'No matter how important his visitors, he would immediately attend mass or matins or evensong as soon as he heard the bell ring that signalled they were about to begin.'[20]

Discipline and leadership

What kind of leader was Prior John? Was he a disciplinarian? We find some answers to these questions in the sources.

'He was very wise and merciful, well considered in judgement and not vengeful, full of pity and good sense.

He was very understanding towards all those, young and old, who were guilty of sins, for he so explained their actions to them that they soon began to see their behaviour for what it was – as he did.

He was so gifted in handling his fellow monks that he could rebuke them without provoking their resentment.'[21]

It seems that often his fellow canons and servants would feel John's restraining hand upon them, as it were from a distance, and they would be checked in whatever doubtful practice they were involved. 'He who was absent in the body seemed in a marvellous fashion to be standing by them in the body and to address and reproach them, so that they might abstain from misdemeanours of this sort.'[22]

Discussions, with advice from the Prior

Capgrave gives various anecdotes which are not found in the other sources, for example, this theological discussion:

'Therefore boiling over with the most loving purposes of God's law, and reading attentively the lives of the most far-sighted fathers, he laid his eyes on that passage of Scripture in which that ancient crafty serpent with his twisted power visited some hermit in visible form. The thread of these words William of Sleightholme of venerable memory observed judiciously. At that time William was chaplain – now indeed with his outstanding holiness and dazzling miracles he gives honour to the same monastery and is an outstanding credit to it – and proposed a portion of this question to the most holy Father: "Concerned as I am about the understanding of the interior man, I am very surprised why this self-same crafty serpent is not seen by men in modern times just as he was in the days of old". John's fatherly good sense quickly resolved the obscurity of this question. "The hearts of the old fathers," said he "were not taken up with empty and sophistic glory, rather they were divinely illumined by the grace of heaven, and recognising the deceitful devices of the cunning enemy, like unbeaten boxers they spiritedly defeated the deadly probing of the enemy."

When amongst such salutary advice he was asked which of the rules was to be carried out most unswervingly, he quickly concluded in the voice of an oracle: "The Gospel of St John," said he, "is far above all rules in the healthiest instruction like a mistress"'.[23]

Prayers and Miracles (*see Appendix E*)

According to all his biographers, John the Prior was responsible for many acts of healing and restoration through his prayers and devotion. There are fifteen accounts of such answers to prayer, including the rescue of sailors at sea and the increase in sheaves in the Great Barn. John himself miraculously survived an accident when a large stone fell on his head, and towards the end of his life he accurately predicted the day and time of his own death.

Of these miracles, the following have been well attested:

Hugo recounts the story of the sailors

'On a certain occasion, when Blessed John was Prior, while five men from the village called Hartlepool in the diocese of Durham were sailing on the sea, a storm came upon them and their boat. The surge of the sea swept over them to such an extent with its swelling waves that it almost overwhelmed them immediately, so that according to reason there seemed to them to be no hope of escape. However, these men, to whom Blessed John was personally unknown, had heard much about his life and his holiness. Seeing themselves in such great danger they began with tearful voices to call on God with one accord, to deign by the merits of the same Blessed Prior of Bridlington to free them mercifully from those very waves of the sea. And while they kept on devoutly praying in this way, behold, there appeared to them someone dressed in the habit of a Canon Regular, who came to them and laying his hand on their boat led them safe to the shore. These men indeed, released from the danger of death in this way, hurried to the monastery as quickly as they could. Immediately they came into John's presence, whom they had not seen anywhere before in the flesh, they went on their knees before him and began to tell in order the whole story of what had happened to them, giving thanks to him for their escape. Blessed John however roundly rebuked them for their words of gratitude, stating that at that time he had been in his monastery. He advised them to keep quiet and go into the church, and there to render devout thanks to God and the blessed Virgin Mary for this reason, and to put nothing down to him, but everything to God, who alone works wonders.'[24]

Five other sources, including the Papal Bull of 1401, contain this story. It is perhaps the best known of all the miracles connected with St John.

Other answers to prayer

Another miracle which is well attested in the sources concerns the supplies of corn and barley:

'Also when corn was in short supply because of the poorness of the soil and high prices, he raised his right hand and blessed it, saying, "May God Almighty

St John's window, All Saints' Church, Thwing

multiply you, because he is powerful". Through John's prayers and merits that corn was so much multiplied, that it supplied the consumption of the monastery for about the next eight months following, though it was estimated that there was only enough for two months. Likewise on another occasion he increased a heap of barley by his merits and prayers; the heap was increased to twice as much and more than had been previously estimated, so that there was enough to make beer for the canons and servants of the monastery and also for whatever else was required for a long time afterwards. All who had seen the barley beforehand were quite amazed at this'.[25]

On another occasion, John himself was suddenly caught up in an emergency which needed a combination of prayer and action:

'Again one night, while Prior John was devoutly concentrating on his prayers, a building within the precincts of the monastery suddenly caught fire; John was almost the first to realise that this happened, and hurried to the spot carrying a big ladder on his shoulders. By himself he raised the ladder and placed it against the blazing building, so that others who came up could climb it and help to save the building. Meanwhile the servants of the monastery and other people ran up, and while they were busy all over the place in order to put out the fire, the Prior gave himself to prayer. Indeed, while he was praying, the fire was suddenly extinguished. Seeing this, those who had come up were very surprised that the fire had gone out so suddenly; indeed, the aforementioned ladder, which the Prior had carried there on his own, three men found it hard enough work to carry back to the place where it had been before'.[26]

John the Prior's last days

As far as we know, John enjoyed good health well into his fifties. However, bouts of the plague were sweeping the country and monastic communities were not immune from such infections. The contemporary historian Thomas Walsingham records that a *Magna Pestis* occurred in the north of England in 1379, the year of John's death.[27]

Canon Hugo describes John's last days:

'John himself foresaw the day of his death in the spirit and knew he was going to move from the world. Round about the feast of St Michael he began to be ill, indicating to certain people who were dear to him and loved as friends that the day of his release was approaching; next after this in the fifty-sixth year of his life he

Chapter 2 / The life of John de Thweng

was seriously attacked by the same illness.[28] He summoned all his brethren into his presence, and made a most holy confession and address to them. He humbly begged pardon from each of them severally, in case he had done anything against them by error or carelessness, uttering words that were so holy, so good and so full of comfort that there was not one of those standing by who could refrain from weeping. Also, when in the presence of their spiritual Father, they humbly begged pardon from him for their transgressions. John himself absolved them, and gave the kiss of peace to all, charging them, begging them and exhorting them to live with one mind and one heart, to continue diligently and fervently in the worship of God, and above all things to love and praise Christ, the generous Giver of all good things. And then, when he had devoutly received the sacraments of the Eucharist and Extreme Unction, right up to the hour of his death, he kept his full understanding, unswerving faith, firm hope, perfect charity and unimpaired memory, such as he had ever had in the days of his health.

Finally, knowing that the hour of his death was approaching, which he had earlier predicted, he gathered together all the canons, his brethren, and in their presence as they stood by, he raised his eyes towards heaven and with the thumb of his right hand he made the sign of the cross on his forehead, on his lips and on his breast, and so holding his hands stretched out towards heaven, and uttering these last words: "Into your hands, Lord, I commend my spirit," as if falling asleep and feeling no pain he most sweetly gave back his spirit to God, on the tenth of October in the year of the Lord 1379'.[29]

Hugo's summary of John's life and work

'Indeed, this blessed Servant of God, throughout the nineteen years or thereabouts in which he was head of the monastery, although he had been very much involved in many tasks to meet the needs of the monastery, still as far as he could made time assiduously for prayer and contemplation. Right until his death, when that blessed soul left the prison of his body seeking the heavens, he led a perfect and most religious life, and shone forth in the greatness of such great merits, as the tongue cannot easily unfold.'[30]

Mention of John the Prior in the Kirkstall Chronicle

In the Chronicle of Kirstall Abbey, a Cistercian monastery near Leeds, we find a short entry about John of Bridlington, written in about 1390, soon after his death and before his canonisation. The author sums up the life of the 'Lord John Thwyng, of sacred memory':

'This same prior, most devout before God, had learnt to glory in the cross of the Lord, and in no other thing, for he was either ascending upward on Jacob's ladder to his Lord by the steps of contemplation, or he was going down on the steps of compassion to his neighbour'.[31]

Chapter 3
The Path to Canonisation

Reports of miracles at the tomb

Soon after the death and burial of Prior John in 1379, reports of miracles at his tomb began to circulate. The historian Thomas Walsingham reported in 1389:

'At that time, in the Priory of canons of Brydlingtone, which is in the diocese of York, at the tomb of John, sometime prior there, miracles so numerous and so manifest were formed that they struck almost all England with amazement; concerning which man they relate that in his life-time he walked on the waters, raised a dead man, and in the barns of his house made such evident and marvellous increase of corn that what was reckoned likely to suffice for the household for scarcely one month, by his prayer sufficed for a whole year; the prerogatives of his sanctity, humility and pity for the afflicted'.[1]

John de Thweng soon became well known amongst senior clergy and members of court, in his own diocese of York and beyond. If it could be proved that miracles had been performed through John, this might lead to his recognition and canonisation as a saint. The family who did most to help the cause of canonisation was the Nevilles of Raby. William Sleightholme, a canon of Bridlington and contemporary of John, was their family confessor, providing a close link with the life of the Prior. There were family links between the Thwengs and the Nevilles; Margery, granddaughter of Marmaduke de Thweng, 'Lord Thweng', was the second wife of Sir Randolph de Neville, 1st Baron of Raby in County Durham. Also, whilst John was still prior, Ralph Neville gave stone for the fabric of the Priory church, sometime before 1367.[2]

In 1386, Alexander Neville, Archbishop of York and a relative of John, commissioned his vicar general Robert Dalton to examine the miracles. Dalton's mandate, sent to the suffragan bishop and others, has survived:

'Snaith July 26, 1386. The prior and convent of Bridlington have told us of the miracles wrought at the tomb of John (de Thweng) their late prior, and urge us to take action in the matter. We desire you to take evidence in the case'.[3]

The report of miracles soon attracted the attention of Richard II, who in 1388, 'on account of his reverence for John de Thweng deceased, late Prior, licensed the

Prior and Convent of Bridlington to surround the Priory with walls and houses of stone and to fortify and crenellate such walls and houses'.[4] The Priory gatehouse, the Bayle, dates from this period. *(See Appendix F for the full text of the licence.)*

In 1390 Pope Boniface IX granted a remission of penance to pilgrims who visited the Priory and/or gave money for the fabric of the church.[5]

In 1391, at the request of Richard II, Pope Boniface asked the Bishop of Palestrina to conduct a similar enquiry into the miracles. This was carried out and, later, the Bull of Canonisation gave a list of the miracles and included details of the background to the investigation:

'We, fully informed, through fitting witnesses and other legitimate proofs, by careful and solemn inquiry and strict examination and discussion, of the sanctity of the life and the truth of the miracles of that saint; these having been found true; and for the sake of the memory of Richard and also of our very dear son in Christ Henry, illustrious kings of England, as also at the frequent and instant request of prelates, nobles, commons, universities and chapters of the said realm; to the glory of Almighty God, the Father, the Son and the Holy Ghost and to the exaltation of the orthodox faith and increase of the Christian religion'.[6]

Canon Hugo lists some of the miracles connected with the tomb of Prior John, including one category which was to make John well known as the patron saint of pregnant women:

'Numerous women, not only from this same province, but also from others, some of whom had been labouring in childbirth for two months and thus were put in danger of death, were saved by calling on St John, and their children gaining the grace of baptism lived for days and years afterwards'.[7]

Hugo finishes his list and his document with a personal touch:

'I am willing to relate in a few words still one more miracle concerning a certain young man, whom I, Master Hugo, know. During the summer season, for what reason I do not know, he became ill. This illness turned into delirium, so that day and night he was extremely distressed and seriously disturbed himself and everyone else around him with his cries and restlessness. There was indeed in that same priory one of Blessed John's birettas, which he used when he was alive. One of the canons who was very devoted to Blessed John took this biretta to the aforesaid sick man and reverently placed it on his head, saying: "May God help you and Blessed John of Bridlington". And without delay the young man I am speaking of who previously had been distressed and restless, began to quieten down and feel better; then he fell asleep and came to himself again with a sound memory, and the following day he was almost restored to health, thanks be to God. However, for the present these things are enough for the recollection of the virtues of that same holy confessor John, Canon Regular, by whose prayers and merits may Christ grant us to come happily to the joys of Paradise. Amen'.[8]

Written records were kept in the Priory

As well as a list of miracles, the Bull of Canonisation contains a short summary: 'For God Almighty by the merits of this kindly confessor opened the ears of the deaf, loosened the tongues of the dumb, to palsied and paralytic limbs gave firm and erect posture, to crippled and lame free gait, sight to the blind, deliverance to those in peril, to other incurable diseases health, brought sailors and those toiling in stormy waters to harbour, and by very many other glorious miracles magnified his saint'.[9]

It would seem that even before the canonisation process was complete, there existed in the proximity of John's tomb at the Priory written records of his life and deeds. These must have been available to visitors and pilgrims, along with various artifacts and even relics connected with the former prior. Again, the Bull states:

'The faithful, however, who are eager to enquire fully into such matters may study them if they consult the authentic books in which the facts are faithfully noted. The votive offerings also placed about the tomb by the faithful in memory of his deeds and miracles and the pictures and other signs set about the tomb, afford a great evidence of the truth of these'.[10]

Capgrave, at the end of his account, says that he has only mentioned some of the miracles connected with St John. 'Indeed, those who are anxious to learn the very many other things that the Lord has worked in our holy patron and incessantly continues to work, will find books in the same monastery in which are described countless kinds of benefit.'[11]

Henry IV supports the cause

Henry Bolingbroke, Earl of Derby, made an offering at Bridlington in 1391 on his return from a crusade in Prussia, and in 1400, when he was king, granted a safe-conduct to John de Gisburne, canon of Bridlington, to visit Rome about the canonisation proceedings.[12] We will see in the next chapter that by the mid-fifteenth century John de Thweng had become the patron saint of the House of Lancaster.

An undated but very early fifteenth century licence under the Privy Seal empowered the prior and convent of Bridlington to send money to Rome in order to pay the fees required by their two proctors at the Roman court for the completion of the process of canonisation of 'J.T. (John Thweng), iadys priour, inasmuch as it has been granted by the Pope'.[13]

The Canonisation

The process was completed on *8 Kal. Oct. 1401*. The volume containing the copy of the Bull in the Vatican Secret Archives is entitled *Bonifacio IX, 1401, Anno 12, Lib 136*. It is a large book made up of parchment leaves, bound in thicker parchment. The entry is in hand-written Latin and occupies ten sides. [See the photograph on page 32.]

The mandate for the 'translation' (removal) of the remains of John the Prior to a new tomb and shrine was dated *7 Kal. Oct. 1401*, i.e. the day before the Bull of Canonisation.

'St Peter's, Rome.
To the archbishops of Canterbury and York, and the bishops of Durham and Lincoln. Mandate to carry out, convoking clergy and people, the translation, desired by the prior and convent of Bridlington, of the body, which lies in their priory, of their sometime prior Blessed John de Thwenge, Confessor, whom, at the often and urgent request of the late king Richard, and of king Henry and other exalted persons, the pope has inscribed in the catalogue of saints, and for whom he has ordered to be celebrated yearly by the universal church the feast and office of a confessor, not a

studio ab omnibus in terris conuenit venerari Et quo solempnius
vt fideles sanctorum colunt memoriam eo dignius eorz patrociniis
proueniunt Nos de sanctitate vite ac veritate miraculorz eiusdem
sancti et aliis pmissis acciosa inquisitionis solempnitate ac districti
examinis discussione p testes ydoneos et alias pbationes legitimas
plenarie informati Huicqz veris compertis et pro pte clare memorie Ricardi ac etiam carissimi in xpo filii nri Henrici Anglie
Regum illustrium vernon et prelatorz prearum et communi vniuer-
sitatim et Capitulorz dicti Regni Anglie et cum instancia requisiti
Ad honorem dei omnipotentis pris et filii et spus sancti et ad exalta-
cionem fidei orthodoxe ac xpiane religionis augmentum auete ipsius
dei omnipotentis ac beatorz Apostolorz Petri et Pauli ac nra
de Fratrum nrorz consilio et assensu omniumqz prelatorum in Romana
Curia consistentium deteruimus declaramus diffinimus et pnuncia-
uimus recolende memorie beatum Johannem Priorem superius
nominatim sanctum esse et tamqz sanctum ab vniuersali ecclia venerari ac scorz Cathalogo ascribi debere et ipm ascribimus de
psenti Statuentes ut ab eadem vniuersali ecclia Anno quolibet
in die qua eius felix anima post deuictum triumphantibz mundum
de carnis libertate tanqz ad astra tendens aulam celestem
adiuit paradisi delicijs feruntur videlicet Sexto ydus Octobris
festum ipsius et Officium sicut pro vno Confessore non Pontifice deuote et solempniter celebretur Et ut ad venerabile sepulchrum
eiusdem gloriosi confessoris feruentius et copiosius xpifidelium co-
fluat multitudo et ipsius celebrius pagatur festiuitas eiusqz no-
men cultrius recolatur auctoritate pdicta omnibus vere penitentibz
et confessis qui sepulchrum huiusmodi apud Bridoratim pdictu
in eiusdem sancti festo deuote visitauerint annuatim ipsius suffragia
petiunt Septem Annos et totidem Quadragenas de iniunctis eis
penitencijs misericorditer velaxamus Quocirca vniuersita-
tem vram monemus requirimus et hortamur attente vobis mandantes
in virtute sancte obediencie et ad eternorum premiorum augmentum
efficacius inuitantes quatinus pntes lras nras cleris et populis
vris auctoritate nra solempniter publicantes festum huius dicti
sancti cum solempnitate debita celebretis et faciatis etiam celebrari
ut pia eius intercessione et hic a nobis psentia et in futuro gaudio
consequi valeatis sempiterna Prestante dno nro ihu xpo qui cum
pre et spiritu sancto viuit et regnat in vnitate deus p infinita secu-
la seculorz Amen Datum Rome apud Sanctumpetrum
Octauo kl Octobr Anno Duodecimo

A page from the 1401 Bull of Canonisation

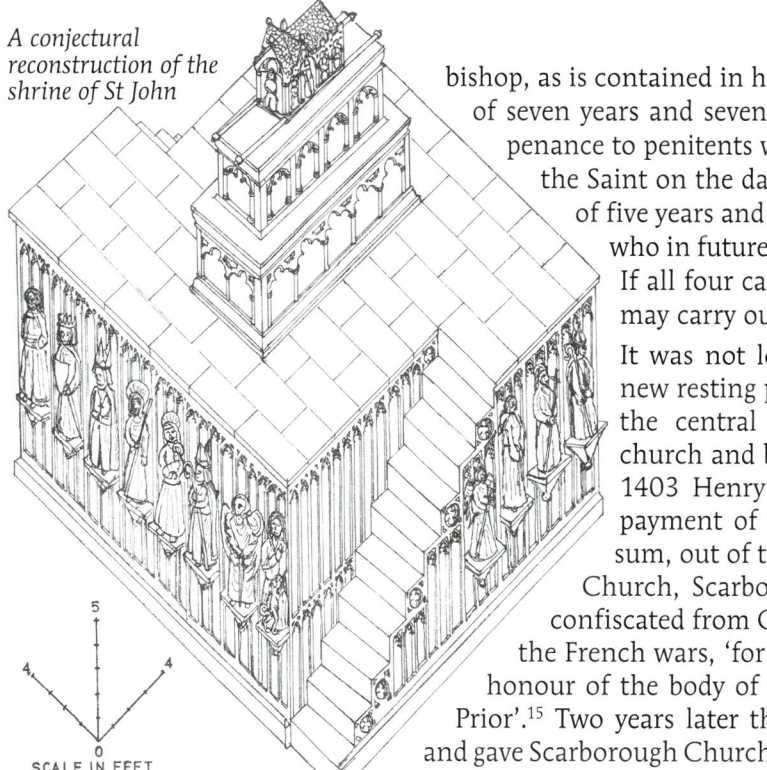

A conjectural reconstruction of the shrine of St John

bishop, as is contained in his letters; with relaxation of seven years and seven quadragene of enjoined penance to penitents who resort to the body of the Saint on the day of the translation, and of five years and five quadragene to those who in future do so on its anniversary. If all four cannot assist, two of them may carry out the translation.'[14]

It was not long before work on the new resting place began, sited east of the central crossing in the Priory church and behind the high altar. In 1403 Henry IV assigned an annual payment of 110 marks, a very large sum, out of the revenues of St Mary's Church, Scarborough, which had been confiscated from Citeaux Abbey because of the French wars, 'for making a new shrine in honour of the body of St John of Thweng, late Prior'.[15] Two years later the king went one better and gave Scarborough Church to the Priory, to become its most valuable possession.

The actual translation to this splendid shrine was carried out on 11th May 1404 by the Archbishop of York, Richard Scrope, and the bishops of Lincoln and Carlisle.[16] The only description we have of the shrine itself comes from Richard Pollard's account of what he found at the Priory when visiting as Henry VIII's commissioner in June, 1537:

'The Reredos at the high Altar representing Christ at the Assumption of our Lady and the 12 Apostles, with divers other great Images, being of a great height, is excellently well wrought and as well gilted, and between the same and the East Window is Saint John of Bridlington Shrine, in a fair Chapel on high, having on either side a stair of Stone for to go and come by.

Underneath the said Shrine be five Chapels with five altars and small Tables of Alabaster and Images'.[17]

Two twentieth-century draughtsmen produced drawings of how the shrine might have appeared from 1404 until the dissolution in 1537. Both were based on a sketch in a burnt fragment of a manuscript in the British Library[18] and on Pollard's description above. Canon Purvis drew the shrine with the entrance and exit to the north and south respectively.

Inscribed picture from the shrine

Priory historian and archaeologist, John Earnshaw, included a drawing of the shrine in his book 'A Reconstruction of Bridlington Priory'. It is thought that some of the shrine's woodwork survived and is now part of the screen in St Oswald's Church, Flamborough. Several inscribed ships are clearly seen there, probably cut by sailors visiting St John's shrine.

Chapter 3 / The path to canonisation

A conjectural restoration of the shrine by J.S. Purvis

St John is added to the calendar

After the announcement of the canonisation in 1401, and the Translation of John's remains in 1404, his popularity spread quickly in both the monastic world and in secular society, amongst royalty, the aristocracy and commoners alike. Not surprisingly, the Augustinian community in England was quick to commemorate their brother canon, now to be remembered as a saint and confessor. The 'General Chapter of all Monasteries of the Augustinian Order (Canons Regular)' which met in Northampton in 1404 issued the following decree:

'Since, then, holy Mother Church has allowed that man venerable and devoted to God, Saint John, formerly prior of the monastery or Priory of Brydlyntone, of our Order, to be written in the number and company of holy Confessors, on account of the merit of his life... and of the plenteous frequency of his miracles... Wherefore... We decree and ordain that the feast of the Deposition of the same Saint John be celebrated on the morrow of St Dionysius, that is to say on the tenth day of the month of October, in all churches, priories or monasteries of our Order aforesaid with solemn festivals for ever in all future times'.[19]

We can imagine this command being obeyed with enthusiasm, especially in the north of England; there were 16 Augustinians houses in Yorkshire alone. In the Missal of Giseburn (Guisborough) Priory, written in 1322 by Walter Hemingford, a canon of that priory, there is a clear addition to the calendar to include St John of Bridlington. It is an exquisitely illustrated book, now in the British Library in London. Under October 10th, John's name is written in black ink on the right of the page, next to that of St Paulinus in red in the left hand column.

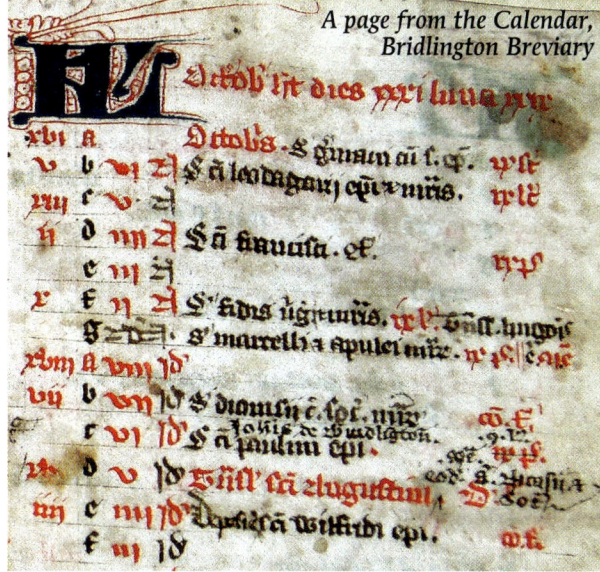

A page from the Calendar, Bridlington Breviary

As to be expected, Bridlington Priory itself would have led the way in the commemoration of St John. The medieval breviary (a service book from about 1380) which is preserved in the Bayle Museum near the Priory church has a very clear entry to that effect in its liturgical calendar. 'Johis de Bridligton' is added between the saints Dionysius (Denys) and Paul (Bishop Paulinus) on October 10th.[20]

As well as entries in monastic calendars, there were a number of Offices of St John (set services for his feast days) in use in Augustinian houses. The complete Office is rare – three copies only have come to light: one for October 10th at Cambridge in Sidney Sussex College Library, another for May 11th in the Bodleian Library, Oxford[21] and an office set to plainsong in the Wollaton Antiphonal, kept in the Nottingham University Library *(see Chapter 4 for more details)*. Other incomplete versions are also in existence, for example in the Guisborough manuscript already mentioned.

It was not only in northern England that John was remembered. His name would have been added to the calendar in monastic houses up and down the country. Examples which survive are from the Brigittine Syon Abbey in Middlesex, the Augustinian Osney Abbey in Oxfordshire, the Augustinian house at Llanthony Secunda, Gloucestershire and the Augustinian Canonesses of Lacock in Wiltshire. He is also mentioned in a Dutch breviary and a Franciscan psalter of Italian provenance in Paris – evidence of how far John's fame spread.

St John also became well-known in dioceses and parishes up and down the country. For example, in March 1405 Bishop Mascall of Hereford awarded an indulgence to those who devoutly visited the church of Llanwarne, between Hereford and Monmouth, or otherwise sent or assigned a free-will offering from the goods God had given them 'out of devotion to the glorious confessor John of Bridlington in whose honour an image of the saint is erected'.[22] That was only a year after John's Translation, and far away from the East Riding.

The Prophecy of 'John of Bridlington'

Tradition attributes the composition of certain Latin political prophetic verses to 'John of Bridlington'. They are couched in obscure symbolism and are concerned principally with English affairs during the reigns of Edward II and Edward III.

The verses of the prophecy are accompanied by an elaborate prose commentary which pretended to untangle the cryptic verses. This commentary, written around 1364, was dedicated to Humphrey de Bohun, seventh Earl of Hereford. The Bohun family were patrons of the Augustinian friars.

Most modern scholarship ascribes the commentary to an Augustinian friar called John Ergome who became master regent and prior of the York convent in 1385. Ergome's library was one of the largest personal collections of the Middle Ages. However, one dissenting scholar has put a strong case for Prior John himself being the author.[23]

On balance, it is doubtful that John de Thweng had anything to do with the composition of these verses and commentary. The Kirkstall chronicler cites the prophecies, attributing them simply to 'Bridlington'.[24] They were used politically by members of the Lancastrian faction and by the supporters of the deposed Richard II. In 1407 two friars and a doctor of Divinity were executed at Tynemouth for using the prophecies to try and show that Richard II was still alive; and in 1403 a hermit, William Norham, was executed in York for apparently predicting the end of Henry IV's reign.[25]

Chapter 4
Pilgrimage and Popularity

By the fifteenth century, pilgrimage had become an important and integral part of religious and cultural life in England. Much interest was shown by people from all walks of life in the saints and their resting places. Saints were seen as miracle-workers and intercessors and so the 'sacred spaces' with which they were associated became popular and much visited. Pilgrims travelled long distances in the hope of a cure or blessing, to fulfil a vow, to deepen their faith and devotion, or simply to see new and exciting places.

Shrines were usually associated with cathedrals, monasteries or significant churches. In the south were those of Thomas Becket at Canterbury and Thomas Cantilupe at Hereford; in the Midlands that of Wilfrid at Repton; in East Anglia that of Our Lady at Walsingham and further north, the shrines of John at Beverley and Cuthbert at Durham.

As well as sites connected to local saints, there were a large number of places where the interest was centred on the Blessed Virgin Mary. Images, pietàs and crucifixes were the focus of devotion at Walsingham, Lincoln, Scarborough, Guisborough, Jesmond and Carlisle.[1]

The availability of relics of the saints always made sites more desirable, as did the granting of papal indulgences. Pilgrims collected souvenirs and badges which proved that they had visited; some pilgrim routes across country became highways, and the hospitality trade flourished at major stopping points and at pilgrimage sites themselves. The most famous description of pilgrimage is found in Chaucer's *Canterbury Tales;* his almost true-to-life characters gathered at the Tabard Inn in Southwark and made their way to Canterbury. In reality, tens of thousands of pilgrims, from kings to peasants, set off to visit holy sites in England during the Middle Ages.

Pilgrims would have travelled to Bridlington from many directions, no doubt using the existing routes. Many of these followed the old Roman roads, the most important of which for Bridlington was that from York to the Humber, which was joined at Market Weighton by the road to Beverley and Hull. In the chronicle of Meaux Abbey, a Cistercian house a few miles north-east of Beverley, there is mention of 'the high road to Beverley' and to 'the royal road which leads from Beverley to the hospital of Routh'. This led north east from Beverley to Bridlington, and then became the coast road to Scarborough.[2] These roads are shown as straight red lines on the Gough map, which dates from about 1360, with a relatively large drawing of a church marking the settlement at Bridlington.[3] The shrines of St John of Bridlington and St John of Beverley were both served by these roads.

Royal Pilgrims to Bridlington

After 1401, St John's fame spread far and wide and Bridlington was placed well and truly on the pilgrimage map. Records have survived which show that a great diversity of people visited the Priory and John's shrine, from royalty and members of the aristocracy, to parish clergy and ordinary people. As a result of such visits, John's popularity grew across the country and abroad.

Certainly, papal support and royal patronage did much to help the cause of St John. Without their aid, what had been a local cult would never have become a national movement. Continuing papal approval of what was happening in Bridlington was demonstrated in 1409 when Pope Gregory XII granted to Prior Thomas and his successors the right to wear the mitre, ring and other episcopal insignia within the Priory and in its churches.[4]

Royal patronage was soon forthcoming from the House of Lancaster. Prince Henry went on pilgrimage to Canterbury in both 1403 and 1407, and, in accordance with an earlier vow, visited Bridlington in May 1408 with Thomas, Earl of Arundel. At that time they were involved in putting down the Welsh rebellion.[5]

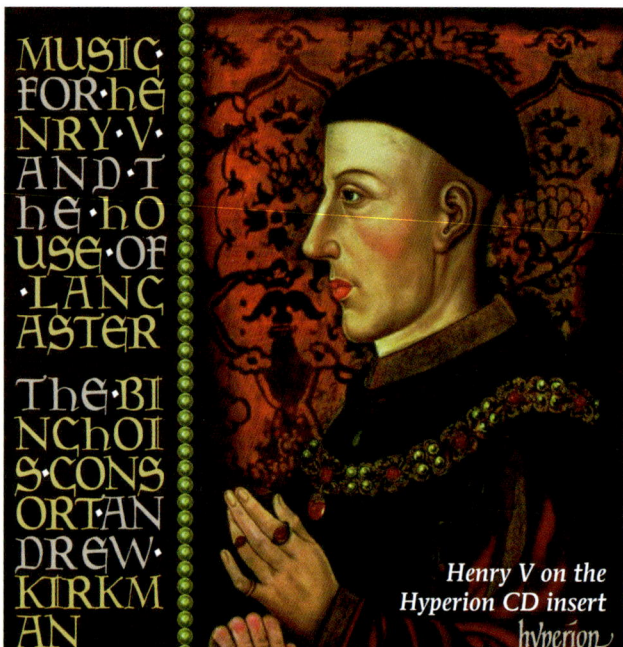

Henry V on the Hyperion CD insert

Henry V named John of Bridlington as his special patron in the will he made in July 1415 before leaving England for the Agincourt campaign, as this extract shows:

'In the name of the most high and undivided Trinity, of the Father, Son and Holy Spirit.

We, Henry, by the grace of God King of England and France, and Lord of Ireland, sound both in body (thanks to the Most High) and in memory, in the matter of our TESTAMENT and of this our last WILL proceed in the following fashion:

First, being about to cross over from this world, Father into your hands I commend my spirit, you have redeemed me Lord God of truth: and, if not by my merits (who am a sinful man), yet I hope that the bosom of Abraham will receive me by the merits and prayer of:

Mary, the most exalted Mother of God,
Saints Michael and Gabriel and all the Angels and Archangels,
Saint John the Baptist and all the Holy patriarchs,
Saints Peter and John and all the Apostles,
Saints George and Thomas and all the Holy Martyrs,
Saints Edward and **John of Bridlington** and all Holy Confessors,
Saints Anne, Mary Magdalene and Brigid, married women,
Catherine, Barbara, Ursula and the Eleven Thousand, and all Holy Virgins,
and all the Court of heaven'.[6]

Thanksgiving for the Victory at Agincourt

Returning to England after Agincourt, late in 1415, King Henry landed at Dover and proceeded to Canterbury. He was met by the Archbishop of Canterbury and all the monks in procession; he alighted at the portal of St Thomas's Church where he offered his prayers, kissed the relics and made his offering. As he arrived in London, the motet *Ave rex Anglorum/Flos mundi/Miles Christi* was performed before the gate to London Bridge to herald the King's entry into the city. He went to St Paul's and adored the Holy Cross, the tomb of St Erkenwald and the high altar 'with great devotion and oblation', before going on to Westminster.

In 1421 the king took his new French wife Catherine of Valois, daughter of Charles VI, on a pilgrimage tour of the kingdom. It was an amazing itinerary: Bristol, through Hereford to Shrewsbury; then Weobley, Kenilworth castle, Coventry and Leicester. Catherine travelled through Hertford, Bedford and Northampton and arrived in Leicester to meet the king on the eve of Palm Sunday.[7] There Henry distributed Maundy money and celebrated Easter. His brother Humphrey, Duke of Gloucester, was also with him.

Together they visited Nottingham, Pontefract and York. Henry went to Beverley and Bridlington without his wife; Catherine was pregnant so stayed behind in York.[8] Sadly, whilst travelling between the two shrines, Henry received news from London of the death in France of his other brother, Thomas, Duke of Clarence.[9]

Despite that news, in Beverley and Bridlington the king gave thanks at the shrines of both St Johns for his victorious campaign in France before continuing the pilgrimage to Lincoln, Walsingham and Norwich.[10]

Henry's companion at arms, Thomas, Earl of Arundel, had not been as fortunate as his royal master. He was invalided home after the Battle of Harfleur and died, at the age of 34, only a few days after he made a new will on 10 October 1415, which included a number of pilgrimage bequests:

'Item, I ordain and will that William Ryman or someone else shall go in my name with all possible haste after my death, on foot from London on pilgrimage to St Thomas of Canterbury, and that two other pilgrimages shall be made, by him or another, on foot from Arundel to St Richard of Chichester, on account of various vows which I made to fulfil personally.

Item, I ordain and will that because of a vow which I made to St John of Bridlington when I was there with the lord king as now is, when he was prince, that every year of my life I would take or send five marks to the said St John, that the arrears due, together with the reasonable costs of whoever is going to go there on this business shall be paid and discharged as soon as possible'.[11]

Two shrines, one pilgrimage

As the fifteenth century progressed, the cults of the two St Johns seemed to merge. With Bridlington and Beverley being only 20 miles apart and having saints with the same name, confusion was inevitable.

It is interesting that St John of Beverley was traditionally regarded as a great helper against the Scots. Athelstan, first king of all England, visited his shrine on the way to Scotland in 934 and carried off the holy banner of the saint as a protection for his army, promising that, if he returned victorious, he would bestow many privileges on the church. He did so accordingly, giving to the church its famous right of sanctuary, and founding a college of secular canons. The banner of Beverley was one of those which floated over the English army at the Battle of the Standard at Northallerton in 1138 when the Scots under King David 1 were defeated by the English under William of Aumale. In the thirteenth and fourteeth centuries, each king of England, going to fight the Scots, borrowed the banner of St John of Beverley from the Minster.[12]

In 1417, however, the Dukes of Exeter and Bedford, hastening to meet the Scots, who were alleged to have made a treaty with Sir John Oldcastle, a Lollard knight,[13] went to Bridlington to venerate St John before fighting with northern troublemakers[14] – an example of how the traditional functions of one saint, protection and healing, were transferred to the other. We might ask – was one saint more effective than the other or was it a matter of local loyalties?

The visits of Henry V must have brought both shrines to the attention of many potential pilgrims and encouraged visits to these towns in the East Riding. At some stage there was co-operation between the guardians of the shrines and a combined pilgrimage badge was issued, probably around 1440. It had two figures – Thweng is depicted as a 'monk' with staff and book, Beverley as a bishop, with a central cross between the two figures. The names *Beuerley* and *Bridlinton* were inscribed across the base.

Amongst other pilgrim badges found in the silt of the river Thames in recent times is one made in the shape of a capital 'B' and having a monk-like figure at the centre – Bridlington and its saintly Prior.[15] This badge formed the basis for the logo of the Priory 900 celebrations in 2013 [see illustrations of badges above].

Other notable pilgrims and supporters

One of the first pilgrims to Bridlington was Margery Kempe of Lynn in Norfolk. She was hardly a typical pilgrim, rather a 'religious professional', devoted as she was to the sacraments and all places and relics connected to the life and death of Christ. Canon William Sleightholme of Bridlington, friend and confessor to John de Thweng, became her adviser and confessor. She made at least two visits to Bridlington; in July 1413 she left York for Bridlington where she visited the shrine and Canon Sleightholme. She returned in September 1417. The list of pilgrimage sites in her autobiography is impressive; it includes Jerusalem, Compostela, Rome, Assisi, Wilsnack and Aachen.[16] Bridlington was among impressive company!

Another notable pilgrim who had a devotion to St John was William Stranton. His story is found in British Library manuscript Royal 17B. He came from Stranton in County Durham, and was familiar with local saints John of Bridlington and Hilda of Whitby. He went on pilgrimage in 1409 to St Patrick's Purgatory on Station Island in Lough Derg, County Donegal, an Augustinian centre. At this place it is said that an entrance to the other world was revealed to St Patrick so that he might more readily convert the pagan Irish. It is recorded that, whilst there, William had a vision, in which he was helped by a guide who was St John of Bridlington. The manuscript contains a miniature showing the saint in his robes, surrounded by several tormenting devils. From the thirteenth century onwards the belief was widespread that whoever spent twenty four hours in the cave on the island would be exempt from purgatory after death.[17]

The window in Morley Church showing St John and St William of York

Bequests to the Priory came from many directions. When the Prince of Wales ousted Archbishop Arundel from the chancery in January 1410, in favour of Thomas Beaufort, he installed Henry Scrope as treasurer and made him a Knight of the Garter. Henry, a nephew of Archbishop Scrope, wrote a will in 1415 in which he made three bequests in memory of St John:

'Item, I BEQUEATH to the bier of St John of Bridlington one collar of gold, with white swans and little flowers, which I have with me.

Item, I BEQUEATH to the Prior of Bridlington, who is alive now, one set of rosary beads, with a silver and gilded crucifix.

Item, I BEQUEATH to the Priory of Bridlington 100 shillings, on this condition: that the whole community in that same place recite Vespers and Matins in the Office of the Dead, and the Commendation of Souls, along with Mass of the Day following for my soul, and that any Canon in the aforesaid Priory should celebrate one Mass, devoutly and specially for my soul, and that afterwards they should have my soul recommended in their chapters'.[18] *(See Appendix C for details from the wills of other benefactors.)*

St John and the Aristocracy

Several well-known aristocratic families took St John for their patron saint as the fifteenth century unfolded. The evidence for this is found in churches in various parts of the country and in surviving examples of Books of Hours, prayer books produced for devout and wealthy families.

One such family was the Beauchamps of Warwick. Richard Beauchamp, Earl of Warwick, had assisted Prince Henry in fighting the Welsh rebellion and had been present at the surrender of Aberystwth in May 1408. He captured Welsh rebel Glendower's banner, and was made a Knight of the Garter. He became a member

of Henry IV's Council, and was High Steward at the coronation of Henry V in 1413.

He took a central role in the dispute with France, and after Agincourt arranged Henry's marriage to the French princess Catherine. Henry V, on his deathbed, gave his infant son, Henry VI, into the care of Richard. This duty required him to travel back and forth between England and Normandy many times. Later he was appointed Lieutenant of France and Normandy, remaining in France for the last two years of his life. He died at Rouen in 1439.

Richard's will, dated 1435, gave detailed instructions for the building of the Beauchamp Chapel at St Mary's Church, Warwick. He was to be buried there before the altar. 'Also I will that there be said every day, during the world, in the aforesaid chapel that, with the grace of God, shall be thus new made, three masses.'[19]

Above: St John in the Beauchamp Chapel window

In that splendid chapel are a number of stained glass windows. To the right of the altar are four figures in glass – St Thomas of Canterbury, St Alban, St John of Bridlington and St Winifred. They were installed in June 1447 and survived the vandalism of puritan troops during the Cromwellian period. More evidence of Richard's devotion to St John and St Winifred is found in his will; he bequeathed his image in pure gold to be offered at the shrines of both saints.

Philip Weller of Nottingham University Music Department writes:

'As major political and administrative players in the affairs of the kingdom, the Beauchamps were a key part of the network of alliance positioned around the House of Lancaster, sustaining it and extending its influence. In such a context, the presence of the 'Lancastrian St John' among a group of English saints that was clearly intended to be representative and emblematic is striking and significant. Partly, the emphasis on English saints was a matter of cultural identity; but it was a question of politics as well. National and regional relationships were being renegotiated during the fourteenth and fifteenth centuries, even as the Hundred Years War and the Wars of the Roses were being played out'.[20]

It is not surprising that St John became a favourite with so many of the well-to-do families of England in the fifteenth century as there were ties through marriage between the Thwengs, Nevilles, Beauforts, Beauchamps and the House of Lancaster.

Books of Hours

Three surviving Books of Hours, all in the British Library, are good examples of this connection with the aristocracy.[21] The 'Beaufort Hours' (Manuscript Royal 2A) contains a beautifully decorated miniature of St John and part of an Office for his feast day. The book was probably produced by Flemish masters and its first owner was John de Beaufort, Earl of Somerset and Margaret de Holland, his wife. The Beauforts, like Henry IV, were descendants of John of Gaunt, Duke of Lancaster.

A miniature of St John in the Beaufort Hours

The second manuscript, the 'Hours of Elizabeth the Queen', dates from about 1430 and contains devotional material relating to St John. It was probably owned by Cecile Neville, the wife of Henry, Duke of Warwick, son of Richard Beauchamp. In 1587 it was used by Mary Queen of Scots before her execution.

The third is the 'Hours of the Blessed Virgin Mary', another lavishly produced prayer book. It was owned by Sir Bertin Entwisle, a hero of Agincourt, and mentions both St John of Bridlington and St John of Beverley.

Additionally, there is a Yorkshire book called the 'Bolton Hours' in York Minster Library; it contains part of an office for the 10th October feast of St John. Lastly, in the Morgan Library in New York is a lavish book, 'Hours of the Virgin for Sarum Use', produced in Rouen in about 1425 for an English aristocrat, Sir William Porter of Lincolnshire. A fine miniature of St John in Augustinian robes is included amongst more than sixty well known saints *(see Appendix B)*.

Music in honour of St John

The Wollaton Antiphonal, an illuminated service book with musical chants, now in the care of Nottingham University Library, was produced in Norfolk for Sir Thomas Chaworth, a wealthy Nottinghamshire magnate, in about 1430. He was related to the Plantagenet-Lancasters through a common ancestor and as a young man had fought with Henry V at Agincourt. He also seems to have had a special allegiance to the Augustinians as he and his wife were buried in Launde Abbey, an Augustinian house in Leicestershire.

The Antiphonal manuscript contains a rhymed office for St John of Bridlington as a special addition, inserted probably around 1440. It includes the only known copy of the plainsong cantus firmus, *Quem malignus spiritu*[22] [see illustration on page 45]. A translation of the Antiphons and Responsory at Matins is as follows:

ANTIPHONS
> *Let the solemn feast of John be worthily celebrated,*
> *that the Son of God may be devoutly petitioned for us.*
>
> *In his youth he blossoms, with already ripened morals,*
> *giving a clear indication, of what may be to come.*
>
> *In order that the flesh might more freely follow the inclinations of the mind,*
> *he enters the cloister, and professes the sacred rule.*
>
> *From a pure model of secular living, the boy, through profession of the rule, is made a canon regular. He exercised different offices of the priory, of which, with industry, he reformed the standing.*
>
> *Light of princes, splendour of the church, solace of the poor, delight of the clergy, may your prayers, father of the church, make us citizens of the heavenly court.*
>
> *Let us rejoice in the Lord who created all things,*
> *and distinguished John with virtue and miracles.*
>
> *May the faithful zealously sing the merits of John*
> *with all due praise, that by his prayers*
> *our debts may be removed at the end of time.*
>
> *Clothed by the Lord in the beauty of virtues,*
> *the convent in concord select him as their prior.*
>
> *Having become prior, he proves to be both Martha and Mary,[23]*
> *loving Rachel before, yet not disdaining Leah.*
>
> *Wise and shrewd, like a serpent, in clemency he ruled,*
> *innocent within, like a dove sighing for its homeland.*

RESPONSORY **Quem malignus spiritu**
> *An evil spirit had seized a possessed man*
> *so intently that he incurred frenzy of mind.*
>
> *Having poured out prayers to the Lord,*
> *he [John] cast out that spirit.*
>
> *And the people, admiring the sign which they had witnessed*
> *as accomplished by the Lord, gave thanks.*
>
> *Having poured out prayers to the Lord, he cast out that spirit.[24]*

As there were five months between the two feasts of St John (of his Translation on 11 May and his death on 10 October), one purpose of the Office was to remind the worshippers of the main events in the life of the saint. This was intended as an aid to worship and celebration.

An anonymous three-part Mass setting in honour of St John was composed in about 1440, based on the *Quem malignus* plainsong. It must have become popular in royal and aristocratic circles in the mid-fifteenth century.[25] Four copies of the mass have survived, the most significant in the so-called Lucca Choirbook, written around 1463 in Bruges, probably for use in the chapel of the English Nation of Merchant Adventurers.[26]

Philip Weller comments:
'The *Quem malignus* Mass was evidently conceived for a skilled ensemble of singers, whose art seems to have left its mark upon the polyphony – its clearness of line, its

sense of rhythmic focus and balance, and the general elegance of its solutions to the problem of presenting the liturgical texts in cogent phrases, while offering at the same time a real sense of articulate musical flow, are all evidence of this. It undoubtedly reflects the professional world of the Lancastrian chapels, and those of the important noble families associated with them (Beauchamp and Beaufort, for example)'.[27]

We know from the inventories of St Mary's Church, Warwick, that by 1465 there was an impressive library of polyphonic music available for services in the collegiate church and Beauchamp Chapel. Earl Richard is frequently mentioned as a donor of some of the most splendid items.[28] It is more than likely that the *Quem malignus spiritu* Mass setting was sung often in that chapel, with the light streaming through the stained glass window depicting St John of Bridlington.

A CD recording featuring the mass was released by the Binchois Consort on the Hyperion label during 2011 (*Music for Henry V and the House of Lancaster*).

As well as the anonymous Mass, there are ten hymns for the feasts of St John still in existence. Three are contained in the Wollaton Office of St John and five are to be found in the comprehensive collection *Analecta Hymnica*, which was published in Leipzig in 1905 and runs to 55 volumes *(see Appendix H and the manuscripts listed in Appendix B)*.

The Wollaton Antiphonal cantus firmus 'Quem malignus spiritu'

Henry VI, St John's relics and the Priory choir school

In 1440 Henry VI founded 'The King's College of Our Lady of Eton beside Windsor' and, a year later, King's College Cambridge, which was to be supplied with scholars from Eton. The school was to be part of a large foundation which included a community of secular priests, ten of whom were Fellows, a pilgrimage church, and an almshouse. Provision was made for seventy scholars to receive free education.

To this end Henry lavished on Eton a substantial income from land and a huge collection of holy relics, among which were fragments of what were supposed to be the True Cross and the Crown of Thorns and also two relics of St John of Bridlington – 'a finger and part of his backbone, which had been given to him by the monks of that convent'.[29] Eton College still has the certificate from Prior

Chapter 4 / Pilgrimage and Popularity

The Priory seal attached to the 1445 relics certificate

Robert Willy stating that he had delivered the relics to Henry VI by the hand of the Duke of Warwick. It reads:

'To all the faithful in Christ to whom these present letters shall be delivered greetings. Know all of you that on the 26th June 1445 we Robert prior of the monastery of Blessed Mary of Bridlington and the convent of the same place on account of the pious and sincere devotion which the most Christian prince our lord the King Henry VI has and shows towards the most blessed confessor John one-time prior of the aforesaid (monastery) have delivered to the same most Christian prince by the hands of the illustrious and powerful lord Duke of Warwick relics of the aforesaid most blessed confessor, namely a joint of one finger and a joint of the backbone of the same (John). In witness whereof my monastic seal has been affixed to the present (letters). Given at Bridlington in our chapter house on the aforesaid day and year' *(see Appendix F)*.

This certificate still has its monastic seal attached. It is identical to one that is to be found on a copy of the Priory Charter in the British Library, a drawing of which is included in Prickett's book on the Priory.[30] There are two figures on the seal, a male and a female; a possible explanation is that the male is St John of Bridlington and the female is the Blessed Virgin Mary.

In 1465 Edward IV obtained papal permission to unite Eton with St George's at Windsor, and the church furnishings and relics were transferred there. The relics were presumably destroyed at the Reformation, as there is no sign of them at Windsor or Eton today.[31]

Henry VI wished St John to be his 'continual advocate at the tribunal of God' and in June 1445 granted the Priory considerable fiscal privileges in return for the daily celebration of mass and recitation of prayers for the well-being of himself and his queen while living, a daily Requiem Mass and a yearly obit after his death. Two years later a further bargain was struck; the Priory extended its services for the good of Henry's soul, and Henry extended the fiscal exemptions and privileges enjoyed by the monastery. On 10th October 1447 the prior sealed an indenture whereby the Priory bound itself thenceforth to maintain 'xij Quaresters and a Maister to teche hem both gramer and song, to admynister at oure Lady Mass daily with note'. As well as singing Mass daily in the Lady Chapel, these boys were to gather each evening after vespers at an image of the Virgin in the Priory church to sing there a votive antiphon to the Virgin, followed by collects, prayers and Psalm 130, De profundis.

Dr Roger Bowers comments:

'The king's part of the bargain was kept on 9th November 1447, when he granted by charter further extensive privileges, both fiscal and at law; in this document the number of boys was given as *six*, and unfortunately it remains unclear whether the choir was to consist of six boys, or twelve. Nothing more is known about this Lady Chapel choir; but few of its kind have their personnel and duties quite so clearly described in documentation of a relatively early date: an instructor and a team of boys, responsible daily for singing Lady Mass and an evening antiphon to the Virgin'.[32]

Above: The St John window in Ludlow Parish Church

In the same year Henry VI, out of devotion to St John, granted permission to the Priory to ship up to 30 sacks of wool free from customs duties, a privilege renewed in 1452, although there is no indication of the port of shipment.

In 1448 the King clearly had the saint in mind again when he issued a charter for the Priory to have three fairs, lasting for three days each, at the Nativity of the Blessed Virgin (8th September) and the two feasts of St John.[33]

Taxes on the Priory were waived by both Henry VI and Edward IV, the latter proclaiming in 1468 'the special devotion of the King to the glorious Confessor St John' *(see Appendix D)*.

Chapter 4 / Pilgrimage and Popularity

St John, seafarers and others

As well as the windows commemorating St John in Bridlington Priory, Thwing Church and the Beauchamp Chapel, three images have survived in other churches:

- A window figure in the chancel of St Laurence's church, Ludlow.
- A window figure in the church of St Matthew, Morley near Derby.
- A painted likeness on the screen in the church of St Andrew, Hempstead-by-Eccles in Norfolk.

The Ludlow window is perhaps the finest of the three St John windows, but its position makes viewing rather difficult. It is high in the large window on the north side of the chancel, in the company of saints Apollonia, George, Leonard, Barbara, Dunstan, Joseph, King David and the Madonna and Child. The glass may well have been the gift of the Clothiers' Guild, although the original inscription has been lost. The date was probably 1450 or 1460.[34] John is depicted as a bishop with mitre and crosier, and the colours of reds and blues are still vivid.

In Morley Church, St John is pictured alongside St William of York in the south chancel chapel. John is shown as a tonsured monk with a pastoral staff in his right hand. He is clothed in a brown habit and blue cloak, not correct for an Augustinian canon. It is a fine window with lovely colours and some coats of arms. It is likely that the local Stathum family, who were related to William, Archbishop of York from 1452 to 1464, had John included due to his popularity at the time. Canon Purvis suggests other historical links in his booklet on St John.[35]

Screen painting of St John in Hempstead Church

Hempstead church is close to the Norfolk coast, about midway between Cromer and Yarmouth. The village is very remote and the church has a thatched roof. The decorated rood screen has eight paintings of saints in eight wooden panels on either side of the central opening into the chancel. The figure of John is between St Denis of Paris and St Giles, although John lived much later than either. Unfortunately his image is badly mutilated following a 'restoration' in the 19th century. The painting is on plaster laid thinly on oak board and there is an attempt to show John in the correct Augustinian dress. Purvis writes, 'The Hempstead figure is important, as it goes to prove the popularity of St John of Bridlington amongst the middle class. The screen was put up, not by a country family in their private chapel, but by the cloth-traders, weavers and farmers of 15th century Norfolk'.[36]

We may wonder how the people of Norfolk had heard about St John of Bridlington. It may well have been through the seafarers of the east coast who traded between Newcastle and the south coast and all ports in between. Bridlington Quay had been under the Priory's control for many years, since the early days of the wool trade which helped to make the community so wealthy. News of John's miracles and of his canonisation would have been carried by sea, as the history of two churches in Kent indicate. Canon Purvis discovered that there had been altars to St John in the churches of St Nicholas, Dover (now demolished) and of St Peter at Sandwich. The entries connected with Sandwich church in a collection of West Kent wills are particularly interesting:

- Light of St John of Bridlington, 4d. John Lacy, 1469.
- A chaplain to celebrate for my soul in the Church of St Peter at the altar of St John of Bridlington for half a year. Ralph Taylor, carpenter, 1475.
- To the Brotherhood of St John of Bridlington, 4d. John Catour, 1485.
- Buried in the Church of St Peter before the altar of St John of Bridlington, near the body of Joan my wife. A priest to celebrate at the same altar for my soul and friends for one year and have 10 marcs. Robt. Richard, 1496.
- To the maintenance of the light of St John of Byrlington, 12d. Robert Broke, 1536.[37]

(in addition, see Appendix C)

Purvis points out that the last entry above shows that services at St John's altar in Sandwich church persisted right up to the time of the Dissolution of Bridlington Priory itself. However, the reference to the Brotherhood is the most intriguing. Despite many searches, no information about the Brotherhood has yet come to light.

The Chapel House at South Molton in Devon presents another puzzle, as very little is known of its history. It was licensed in 1449 as a chantry chapel and dedicated to St Anne and St John of Bridlington.

Later Pilgrimages to Bridlington

For how long did Bridlington hold its place among the great pilgrimage centres of England? Certainly to the end of the fifteenth century, as is indicated by a number of 'last wills and testaments'. There are two good examples: in 1466, William Boston, chaplain of Newark, left 26s. 8d. for a priest to go to Bridlington, Walsingham, Canterbury and Hailes on his behalf.[38]

The list of intended pilgrimages in the 1472 will of William Ecopp, rector of Heslerton, starts in the south and works its way north:
'To Thomas of Lancaster, St Saviour of Newburgh, the Blessed Virgin Mary of Scarborough, St Botulph of Hackness, the Crucifix of Thorpbasset, Blessed Mary of Guisborough, St John of Beverley, St John of Bridlington, St William of York, Blessed Mary of Jesmond, Blessed Mary of Carlisle, and St Nonian in the church of Candida Casa in Galloway'[39] *(see also Appendix C)*.

Chapter 4 / Pilgrimage and Popularity

Map showing places connected with St John of Bridlington

● **Early life of John de Thweng:**
Thwing near Bridlington
Kilton Castle, Cleveland
Oxford University

● **Manuscripts at:**
Guisborough, Cleveland
Syon, Middlesex
Osney, Oxford
Lacock, Wiltshire
Llanwarne near Hereford
Llanthony Secunda, Gloucestershire
Kirkstall, W. Yorkshire
Bodleian Library, British Library & Cambridge libraries
Durham Cathedral Library
Wollaton, Nottingham
York Minster Library

● **Stained glass windows at:**
Warwick
Ludlow
Morley near Derby

Miscellaneous Connections:
● Painted screen image at Hempstead, Norfolk.
Chapel dedicated to St John and St Anne, South Molton, Devon
Eton College, Windsor.
St Patrick's Purgatory, Lough Derg, Co. Donegal.
Pilgrim badges found in silt on the banks of the River Thames, London.
Altars and petitions at Dover and Sandwich.
Beverley shrine.

Chapter 5
The Legacy of St John

We have seen that the fifteenth century was a time of prosperity and stability for Bridlington Priory. A considerable number of pilgrims visited the shrine of St John and the Priory received an enviable list of royal privileges and special gifts.

In complete contrast, the following century was to bring destruction and pillage on an enormous scale, carried out in the name of Henry VIII and with his full authority. The dissolution of the monastery at Bridlington in 1537 changed this coastal community for ever.

The Lords Feoffees established

The Priory nave escaped destruction and continued to serve the community as the parish church of St Mary. However, the local lands of the Priory and the harbour were let on lease to various individuals, but remained the property of the Crown. The cost of repairing and maintaining the harbour proved to be high; this became a long-standing problem and the subject of controversy. In 1591, in the reign of Elizabeth I, the manor and rectory were leased to John Stanhope Esq. who had the responsibility for providing a priest for the parish. In 1624 Sir John Ramsey, the Earl of Holderness, was granted the manor by King James I.

After Ramsey's early death his brother took over, but soon the manor was sold to thirteen inhabitants of Bridlington who later became the first Lords Feoffees. This transaction was confirmed by Charles I and with the signing of the Great Town

The Bayle gatehouse today

The Priory Choristers celebrating their RSCM awards in 2011

Deed in 1636 many townsfolk who were tenants were able to contribute and buy their properties, so becoming freeholders. The Lords have continued to this present day to have oversight of the Manor of Bridlington. They are elected for life, Assistant Feoffees stepping up to become full Lords.

The patron of the living at the Priory was the Archbishop of York until the end of the 18th century when it was transferred by act of Parliament to the Revd Matthew Buck and his heirs. This responsibility was taken over by the Simeon Trustees in 1835. The Priory was the sole parish church of the town until increases in both residents and visitors necessitated the building of more churches – Christ Church and Holy Trinity in the 19th century and Emmanuel Church in the early 20th century. Gradually other denominations had built their own churches, and ecumenical co-operation became a hallmark of the Bridlington churches, each working wherever possible with partner churches.

The great monastic themes today

As we reach 2013 and the 900th anniversary of the founding of the Priory, our attention is drawn to the three great monastic themes, so evident in the life of Prior John de Thweng, and the ways in which they are still being lived out today. Here is the real legacy of St John:

PRAYER
- **Public worship**: the day at the Priory begins with Morning Prayer using the 'Daily Prayer' liturgy in Common Worship. There are three services on Sundays, two of which are Eucharistic. On Wednesday afternoons there is 'Prayer for the Parish' followed by a said Communion. 'All-member ministry' means that many members of the congregation are regularly involved in leading worship.
- **Private prayer**: the church is open daily and the Chapel of St John is available for quiet intercession and contemplation. Cards with prayer requests can be left there and the votive candle stand is adjacent to the chapel.
- **The choral tradition**: the Priory has a full robed choir with boy trebles and sings at two services each Sunday under the direction of a professional

choirmaster and with the support of a deputy organist. The choristers receive many spiritual, musical and social benefits from their time in the choir, as they in turn enhance the worship and witness of the Priory.

- **Prayer for healing and wholeness**: following the visit in 1999 of Russ Parker, Director of the Acorn Christian Healing Foundation, prayer for healing has been offered at the three main Eucharists each month. The Chapel of St John is used, very appropriately, for this ministry.

STUDY

- **Schools**: following the establishment of the Priory choir school in 1447, the Priory continued to be involved in the provision of local schools. Hustler's Free Grammar School was founded in 1636 and the National School (a church foundation) in 1826. Bridlington School was founded in 1899 but traces its origins back to the 1447 choir school founded by Henry VI.

  Today the Priory has close links with Bridlington and Headlands secondary schools and with the four primary schools – Burlington Infants and Juniors, New Pasture Lane and Bay.

- **Biblical foundations**: the Priory has always emphasised the reading of Scripture and Biblical preaching. The Simeon Trustees, as patron of the living, have continued to help maintain that tradition.

- **Christian education**: as well as encouraging the choristers in their faith, the Priory runs other children's activities. The 'Priory Lights' group meets on two Sunday mornings each month and plays a part in the Family Services. Special workshops are organised at Christmas and Easter.

  For adults there are annual Lent courses and the Emmaus course. There are currently two Cursillo study groups and a meditation group which meet on a regular basis.

- **Christian literature**: the Priory Shop stocks a number of Christian books and Bible study notes are also available, all with the support of the Bethany Christian Bookshop in the town.

HOSPITALITY

- **Services for community groups**: annual services include the Great Gale service in conjunction with the local RNLI branch, the Civic Service, the Combined Ex-service Association's service, carol services for local schools and the annual 'RE Action' days organised with the East Riding Council. Special services are also held as part of the Old Town Festival and the Bridlington Arts Festival.

- **Rites of Passage**: baptisms, weddings and funerals are held as required for those who live in the Priory parish, and sometimes for those from further afield.

- **Community events**: concerts and other musical events, including the annual organ recital series, are often in the Priory calendar. Ecumenical musicals have been staged in the Priory and the East Yorkshire College prize-giving is an annual event.

- **The church is open daily:** visitors are assisted by members of the Priory Guild of Stewards. Maps showing the location of the Thompson mice on the oak furniture are available for children (carved wooden mice are the trademark of Thompsons of Kilburn).
- **Compassion and pastoral care**: the Priory pastoral team visits the sick and lonely in home and hospital. There is a weekly Luncheon Club for the elderly and tins of food are collected for the Bridlington homeless project. The bereaved are supported by the Epiphany Group.

The Priory Family adopted the following Mission Statement in 2002:

Bridlington Priory exists:
- ◆ to worship God, through Christ, in the power of the Holy Spirit,
- ◆ to provide a warm welcome for all who come through its doors,
- ◆ to be a witness in the local community to God's redeeming love in Christ,
- ◆ to serve that community in love,
    working wherever possible with partner churches as members of 'Churches Together in Bridlington and District'.

In conclusion – the real Prior John?

The medieval life stories of St John and the enduring legacy of his time at the Priory combine to paint a picture of the real man. He comes across the centuries as a very human character, humble and vulnerable but also spiritually strong and inspired.

He was first a man of prayer, under whose leadership the Priory flourished as a centre of worship and healing. Connected with that was his study of the Scriptures and his special love for the Fourth Gospel as the guide to Christian discipleship. At all stages in his monastic life John 'practised what he preached', both in how he ran the monastic community and how he and his fellow canons served the local people in their practical and spiritual daily needs.

As the Middle English author writes, 'Truly the story of his life should have a good influence on those who hear it'.

The Priory West End today

NOTES
(See Appendix B on page 63 for details of abbreviations)

Chapter 1

1. Martin, T.F.: *Our Restless Heart*, DLT, 2003, chs. 1 & 2.
2. Southern, R.W.: *Western Society and the Church in the Middle Ages*, pp. 241-2.
3. Brid. Chart., p. 12, "Carta fundatoris Monasterii de Bridelington". See also Prickett, p. 65.
4. Victoria County History, East Riding, ii, pp. 14, 30.
5. Jennings, B.: *Yorkshire Monasteries*, p. 1.
6. See Jennings, op. cit. ch. 6.
7. Prickett gives a list from Bishop Bale of the 21 books written by Robert the Scribe (Appendix G., p. 86).
8. BL, Harley MS 50.
9. Dialogue, VIII, p. 101a.
10. Dialogue, VIII, pp. 100a-101a.
11. Dialogue, Introduction, p. xvi.
12. Dialogue, Prologue, p. 4a.
13. All capital letters in the translation correspond to capitals in the original Latin text.
14. Dialogue, p. xxiva.
15. Jennings, op. cit. p. 117; The Chronicle of the Canon of Bridlington, RS 76, vol. II, pp. xvii-xxxi; The Chronicle of Peter of Langtoft, RS 47.
16. Neave, David & Susan: *Bridlington, an introduction to its History & Buildings*, Smith Settle, 2000, p. 10.
17. Neave, op. cit. p. 5.

Chapter 2

1. Hugo, I, 1.
2. Hugo, I, 1.
3. Capgrave, p. 64.
4. Ashby, note 3.
5. Hugo, I, 3.
6. Prickett, pp. 27-28. The chalk slab bearing the name and date of Prior Robert is still to be seen in the Priory (see Lamb, J.W.: *A Guide to Bridlington Priory Church*, p. 24).
7. ME Verse, 22.
8. Hugo, I, 6.
9. Hugo, II, 8.
10. Hugo, II, 9.
11. Capgrave, p. 70.
12. Hugo, II, 11.
13. Hugo, II, 10.
14. Ashby, Gielemans, 2.
15. ME Verse, 48.
16. ME Verse, 41, 42.
17. Capgrave, p. 72.
18. ME Verse, 43, 44.
19. see Hugo, III, 18.
20. ME Verse, 43, 44, 47.
21. ME Verse, 50, 25, 26.
22. Hugo, II, 16.
23. Capgrave, pp. 8-9.
24. Hugo, III, 17.
25. Hugo, III, 21.
26. Hugo, III, 20.
27. WHA, I, p. 409.
28. Capgrave, p. 77, has 'in the sixtieth year of his age' which fits better with the other dates in John's life.
29. Hugo, III, 22, 24, and footnote (h).
30. Hugo, III, 24.
31. Kirkstall, p. 55.

Chapter 3

1. WHA, vol II, p. 189, translated by Purvis.
2. Hughes, J.: *Pastors and Visionaries*, p. 99n.
3. RS 61, CCLXII, p. 420.
4. Brid. Chart, p. 11.
5. Jennings, op. cit. p. 128.
6. Purvis, p. 41.
7. Hugo, IV, 26.
8. Hugo, IV, 28.
9. Purvis, p. 40.
10. Purvis, p. 41.
11. Capgrave, p. 78.
12. Rymer, Foedera viii, 4 October 1400; CPR, p. 439.
13. BL, Add. MS. 24,062, fol. 7v; Twemlow, J.A., *A Miscellany*, 1914, pp. 128-131.
14. LR97, pp. 455-461.
15. CPR, Henry IV, 1401-1405, p. 248.
16. WHA, vol II, p. 262.
17. Prickett, Appendix O.
18. BL, Cotton MS, Vitellius E.
19. Purvis, p. 80: *Chapters of the Augustinian Canons*, CYS, C. fol 62.
20. Parsons, Anna: *The Bridlington Breviary*, part of her Exeter University PhD thesis, July 2004.

21 See the Purvis Office.
22 Registrum Roberti Mascall, 1404-1416, ed. J.H. Parry, CYS, pp. 15-16.
23 Rigg, George: Speculum 63, 1988.
24 Curley, Michael J.: *Oxford Dictionary of National Biography*, 'John of Bridlington'.
25 Hughes, op. cit. p. 361; WAC, p. 231.

Chapter 4

1 Webb, D.: *Pilgrimage in Medieval England*, p. 103.
2 Webb, op. cit., pp. 229, 300n. *Chronica Monasterii de Melsa*, ii, pp. 92, 108.
3 see http://www.goughmap.org (the manuscript is in the Bodleian Library in Oxford).
4 Jennings, op. cit. p. 129.
5 WAC, p. 25; Register of Henry Chichele, CYS ii, 74.
6 Rymer's Foedera with Syllabus: July 1415, Volume 9, pp. 283-298 (extract, translated by Gerald Moxon).
7 'Die parassenes', PRO: E 403/646, m.13.
8 'intime' PRO: E 403/646, m.1.
9 Allmand, C.: Henry V, London, 1992, pp. 33, 158.
10 WHA, Vol. II, pp. 335, 337; Wylie: *The Reign of Henry V*, iii, pp. 270-272.
11 as note 5 above.
12 Dresvina, Juliana: *St John of Beverley, St John of Bridlington – Blurring a Border between Two Saints' Cults*.
13 The Lollards were followers of John Wycliffe, a critic of the Catholic Church and leading reformer.
14 WHA, vol. II, p. 325.
15 Spencer, B.: *Pilgrim Souvenirs & Secular Badges*, 1999, pp. 194-196.
16 Webb, op. cit. pp. 205-206. Hughes, op. cit. p. 238.
17 Easting, Robert, ed.: *St Patrick's Purgatory*, EETS, 298, 1991, pp. 77-117.
18 Rymer op.cit., pp. 258-283 (extract, translated by Gerald Moxon).
19 The Collegiate Church of St Mary, Warwick: *The Beauchamp Chapel*, 1997.
20 Weller, Philip: *Music for Henry V and the House of Lancaster*, a CD by Hyperion, 2011.
21 See Appendix B, British Library Manuscripts.
22 WA, ff. 411-413.
23 See introductory comment in chapter 1 on Martha and Mary as monastic archetypes.
24 Translation by Philip Weller (see note 20 above).
25 QMS: 2. Mass *Quem Malignus Spiritu*.
26 See note 20 above.
27 See note 20 above.
28 Bowers, Roger: *Choral Institutions*, part 5. PhD thesis, University of East Anglia, 1975; 5.3.1.B.
29 Lyte, C. Maxwell: *A History of Eton College, 1440-1875*, MacMillan.
30 BL, Harley MS 44. B.2. Prickett (1831 ed.), pp. 18, 80 and Plate XI.
31 Hatfield, P., Eton College Archivist, email dated 27 September, 2011.
32 Bowers, op. cit. 5.2.4.A (CChR 1427-1516, p. 118).
33 Jennings, op. cit. p. 129.
34 Purvis, pp. 8-9.
35 Purvis, p. 5.
36 Purvis, p. 11.
37 Duncan, LL: *Testimenta Cantiana*, 1906, pp. 289-290.
38 TE, vol. II, p. 283.
39 TE, vol. II, pp. 200-1.

GLOSSARY OF TERMS

Antiphon – an acclamation said or sung before and after a canticle during the office, usually to mark a festival or season in the Church's year (see *Propers*).

Antiphonal – an office book containing chants and psalms which were designed to be sung by groups on alternate sides of the church, i.e. antiphonally.

Augustinians – followers of the Rule of St Augustine (354-430 AD), canons living in a community, usually ordained priests.

Benedictines – followers of the Rule of St Benedict (c480-c550), monks living in community.

Breviary – a service book containing prayers, hymns and psalms, for use at Divine Office rather than at the Mass.

Cantus firmus ('fixed song') – a pre-existing melody forming the basis of a polyphonic composition, e.g. the three-part Mass setting.

Cistercians – an order formed from a group of Benedictine monks in 1098, having the aim of adhering more strictly to the Rule of St Benedict. They founded many houses in England, including Fountains Abbey.

Commemoration – an act of remembrance of the saints, usually involving additions to the normal offices or Mass (see *Antiphon* and *Propers*).

Convent – a community of canons, monks or nuns living together under a common rule. The restricted use of 'convent' for a female community is not historical.

Dominicans – friars of the Order of St Dominic (preachers).

Mass – the central service of the Christian Church in which the Last Supper, the Crucifixion and Resurrection of Christ are recalled. It is also called Communion or the Eucharist, meaning 'Thanksgiving'.

Missal – a service book for use at Mass.

Office – a regular service, said or sung, which forms part of the daily worship in a Christian community.

Opus Dei – the daily monastic cycle of offices and Mass ('The Work of God').

Plainsong – an unaccompanied chant sung in unison, used for singing psalms, canticles and antiphons.

Profession – the ceremony when a new canon, monk or nun makes vows for life.

Propers – additional prayers, chants and readings for a special occasion, e.g. a saint's day. These are placed within the regular offices or Mass of the day.

Relics – bodily remains or any personal memorial of a saint, considered to be holy and connected in the popular opinion of the times with miracles and answers to prayer.

Responsory – a said or sung part of a service which can occur several times in any given act of worship, often before and after psalms or canticles. It provides greater participation in the liturgy for the congregation.

Translation – the removal of the remains of a saint and their re-burial in a new tomb, usually within a church building.

Appendix A

The Middle English Verse Life of Prior John
With a translation into modern English by Nicky Terry.

Who that lufes or likes to here,
Of gude mens lifes that are has bene,
Be thame ensample may thai lere,
Here for to life bothe wele and clene.

1. Whoever loves or likes to hear about the lives of good men, who have lived in years gone by, may learn by their example to live good and innocent lives at this present time.

Bot now be on that had no pere,
Whils that he lifed is that I mene,
His name is knawen bothe fer & nere,
And I myself I haue hym sene,
The gude prior of Bridlyngtonne,
A hale man of religion,
And als of gude perfeccion.

2. But now (to speak) of one who has no equal – I mean during his life-time – one whose name is known far and wide – one whom I myself have seen – a holy man of religion and a blameless life – the good Prior of Bridlington.

Sothely to speke of his lifyng,
Thai that wil here it mai thame mend,
Yit wald he nouthir ald ne ying,
Of his dedis be aknawen ne kend,
Withoute fagyng or glosyng.

3. Truly the story of his life should have a good influence on those who hear it – yet he would not wish anyone old or young to be instructed about his deeds without explanation.

Al that I knew to his lifes end,
I may shew as it is Goddis biddyng,
Aftir the dede man to commend,
For he that takes a gude purpose,
Of weledoyng he may not lose,
And thataftir wil hym dispose.

4. I may tell all I know of him to the end of his life, as it is the will of God to praise a man after death, for who has good intentions to do well, cannot lose and thereafter will be at God's disposal.

This name of John for to discrife,
Is called the grace of God be right,
Slike grace als he had in his life,
Thar is now few that tel it myght.

5. There are few who can tell or give an account of the life of this man called John, chosen by the grace of God which remained with him all his life.

He began tymely well to thrife,
And serue God bothe day and nyght,
Als sely barne is lerned belife,
Thrugh his grace that was in him light,
For allway fro begynnyng,
Of his childehed to his endyng,
Bot of his God and weldoyng.

6. From his early years he thrived and began to serve God day and night and this happy/innocent child learned to believe, through the grace bestowed on him, in God and goodness from his childhood to his life's end.

For truly whils he was a childe,
To no lightnes he wald assent,
Bot was ay sobir, meke, and mylde,
And to his lare gaue gude intent.

7. For, during his childhood, he had no truck with levity but was always serious and gentle and devoted to his studies.

When odir childer that were wilde,
To thare playing fro the scole went,
With fulehed he ne wald be filde,
Bot lifed ay als an innocent;
At softly he wald stele tham fra,
And to the kirk fast wald he ga,
Whare he was ay occupied swa.

8. When other high-spirited children left school to play, he had nothing to do with foolishness, but always behaved well. He would steal away from them and go quickly to the church where he was always spending his time.

Right as a tre begynnyng is to bew,
Tymely that gude camboke wil be,
In al that men myght se or knew,
Fro his youthed right so did he.

In his youth vowed chast ful trew,
And forsoke all dishoneste,
That in his life be signes knew,
And eftirward men myght it se.

For when that men vnto hym pray,
He berys it forth to God allway,
Thus here I tell full many say.

For fro the tyme that he couthe gude,
Hafand witt and discretion,
On ane purpas sadly he stude,
At be man of religion.

Perseuerant hale in that mode,
Forthi with grete deuocion,
To Bridlyngton at last he yode,
And was receyued there a chanon;
Thame thoght he suld be graciouse,
And there to hym thai graunt the house,
Thus he become religiouse.

Pompe and pride and couetise,
With hert & will here he forsoke,
And odir vices on all wise.

Gifand hym sadly to his boke,
Hymself and the warld to despise,
He lerned be that he vndirtoke,
To spende his tyme in Goddis seruice.

When odir slepe ful oft he woke,
Prayand to God ful besily,
Lifand wele and religiously,
Vnto the kirk ay first redy.

And thus fra that he was profest,
He kepte hym oute of syn & shame,
And to gude company hym kest,
And did so that he hd no blame.

Commune lifyng thoght him the best,
Sauand ay wele here his gude fame,
He serued God in ese and rest,
And thus began his nobil name.

He was wel taght and manerly,
And couth hymself ful felawly,
In worde and dede meke and esy,
Stedfast, true, witty, war, and wise,
Of fair maners honest and hende,
[Tham] at wele did at dyuyse,
He couth be both felaw & frende.

9. Just as a young tree early shows signs of good growth and future development, so could the signs of future holiness be observed in him.

10. In his youth he vowed to be chaste and avoided all things dishonourable – these qualities were in his way of life, and witnessed by others as he grew up.

11. When people pray to him for help, he passes on their requests to God as many can bear witness.

12. For from the time that he acquired understanding of the good, he was seriously devoted to one purpose, having both intelligence and discretion – to be a man of religion.

13. Therefore with great devotion, never slackening in his determination to pursue this course, he eventually went to Bridlington, where he was received as a canon. There they thought him favoured and granted him a house and so he became a monk.

14. Here he gave up pomp, pride and love of money and property and all other vices.

15. Devoting himself seriously to his learning, he learnt, by that way of life he had chosen, to reject worldly values and to be humble and to spend his time in the service of God.

16. Often, while others slept, he would be awake, praying earnestly to God and, living a good and religious life, he was always the first to be ready to attend church.

17. And so from the time he was professed, he avoided all evil and shameful behaviour and kept good company, so that no blame attached to him.

18. He enjoyed community life to the full, serving God in peace and contentment and so his good reputation began to grow.

19. He was well-educated and knew how to behave correctly and was very friendly, conducting himself in speech and action with ease and self-control – reliable, honest, intelligent, perceptive and wise – honourable and courteous in his dealing. He knew how to be both companion and friend.

Prayand him that is prince of pris,
Fro alkyns vice he sulde hym shende,
And so he ouercome his enmys,
The warld, the flew, & eke the fende.

That was a ful grete victorie,
As the boke says that cannot lye,
For who of thame may get mastrye.

He was a man of fair stature,
Louely and semely on to see,
And ther withall coy & demure,
Of all gude he was hauand plentee,
Forthy he was supprioure,
Worthy to gretter dignite,
That shewed he when he had the cure,
For he did ilk man equite.

He myght wele suffir & abide,
Seand mens dedis on ilk a side,
Wham that he knew wel occupied.

He was so gude ay manyfald,
Be grace that God gan to him lend,
In his lifyng who wilde behald,
It was ensaumple to all men.

He was full aghfull yong & ald,
To thame that trespast then & then,
Fro he thar parte to tham had tald,
Thai began sone thamself to ken.

He couthe blame men so skilfully,
That thai to him had none enuy,
Whoso was in his company,
Off cloisterers hauand kepyng.

What that he taght, first he it did,
He gaf insample in al thing,
The bettir he myght teche & bid,
He gafe gude kepe to weldoyng.

So kynde and curtase was he kyd,
God wald that he had worshipyng,
That his gude name ne wer not hid.

Thare was he tane to mare honoure,
And maugre his chosen prioure,
Of his lifying he was meroure.

When he was put vnto that degree,
Agayn his will and made prelate,
He kest hym meker for to bee,
And had no pride of his astate,
Hymn thoght it bot a vanite,
And lifed als ane of thame God wate,
And was in perfite charite,
Vnto all men that I wel wate.

If any man trespas had done,
Askand mercy he forgafe sone,
He was not wrath with thar persone.

20. Praying to Him who is Lord of all, that He would destroy in him all manner of vice, he overcame his enemies – the world, the flesh and the devil.

21. As is stated in the Bible (the book that cannot lie), that is a very great victory – for who is able to overcome them.

22. He was a handsome and attractive man, quiet and well-mannered and full of goodness, for which reason he was appointed sub-prior and was worthy of higher office, as was proved when he achieved the responsibility, for he dealt justly with everybody.

23. He might well wait patiently, observing the deeds of all around him as they went about their business.

24. By the grace of God he did so many good deeds in his life that he was an example to all who would observe him.

25. He was very understanding towards all those, young and old, who were guilty of sins, for he so explained their actions to them that they soon began to see their behaviour for what it was – as he did.

26. He was so gifted in handling his fellow monks that he could rebuke them without provoking their resentment.

27. He practised what he preached and took great care to provide an example of good living, so that he might be a better teacher and director.

28. He was known to be so kind and courteous that it was the will of God that he should be respected and that people were aware of his good reputation.

29. There he was accorded more honour and in spite of his chosen life as prior, he was famous in the eyes of both learned and ignorant.

30. When, against his will, he was made prior, he tried to be more humble and took no pride in his position, for he considered worldly status worthless and he continued to live as one whom God knows, and was in perfect charity with all men – for that I well can vouch.

31. He was quick to forgive any sinner who asked for money, and was not angry with that person.

Thof he fro the warld was ay drawand,
And tuke that charge not with his will,
Of many thingis he was conand,
And couthe thame bring to gude be skill.

He was ful shew and dredand,
That oght in his tyme suld fair ill,
Bot God sent vertu in his hand,
That all gude thrift fell him vntill.

He gaf hym so to Goddis louyng,
That in his dais for wele al thing,
And it is like in tyme comyng.

He was bothe wise and amyable,
And couthe wel here & se & layne,
In his beryng sad and stable,
He spake ne did right noght in vayne,
What that he said was acceptable,
For it was fonde the best, certayne,
Forthi he was ful prophetable,
In slike a hous to be souerayne,
For he wald noudir chide ne flite,
Nor in his hart had no dispite,
In God was haly his delite.

He ordaynd so for thingis inward,
That God was serued faire & wele,
Therfore al thing that was outward,
Thai fure the bettir ilk a dele.

Of his hauyng he was not hard,
Bot sauand and ay true als stele,
Who that gude did to his housward,
He quyt tham so that thai myght fele.

He was discrete, gude of counsaile,
Worthi to haue gret gouernaile,
Lufand his God withouten faile.

It was ful mekil wittirly,
Of two gret charge haue besynes,
That is to say of thing wardly,
With odir spiritual thingis that es.

He did bothe ful auysidly
Lifand als his dedis beres witnes,
And yit knew none that was him by,
That euer he serued God the les;
For thrugh the grace of the Haly Gaste,
He wald no tyme here in vayn waste,
Bot gostely thingis ay vsed he maste.

He was bothe large and liberall,
Of mete and drink and almose dede,
And that mainly to pouerall,
For thame he wald both clethe & fede,
Also mercyfull to all,
That mystir had to hym in nede,
Souerayn help he was ouer all,
To all degrees he tuke gude hede.

32. Although he was an unworldly person and reluctant to bear office, he had wide knowledge of many things and had the skill to act wisely and well.

33. He was considerably fearful that things might go wrong during his time in charge, but God granted him such ability that all was managed successfully.

34. He so gave himself to the love of God, that all went well in his life-time and was likely to do in the future.

35. He was both wise and kind, and well known to be everywhere steady and firm in his behaviour. His good words and deeds were not in vain, but what he said was certainly accepted as the best and therefore he was well suited to rule such a religious house, for he would neither scold nor criticise. He had no malice in his heart and his whole delight was in God.

36. He so ordered the life of the monks that God was served honestly and well; therefore all outward undertakings fared the better.

37. He did not cling tightly to his possessions, but saved responsibly and with complete honesty *(true as steel)* and he repaid completely any good done to the monastery.

38. He was discreet and a wise counsellor, fit for a position of power, constant in his love of God.

39. It was indeed a massive responsibility to have two great tasks simultaneously – temporal and spiritual.

40. He managed both tasks efficiently, as his manner of life bears witness, and no one who knew him felt that he served God any less well *(because of his other responsibilities)* for, through the grace of the Holy Spirit, he never wasted time but devoted himself most to spiritual matters.

41. He was both liberal and generous in distributing food and drink – and in works of charity and that especially to the poor, for he would both feed and clothe them. Also he showed mercy to all who approached him in their need. He was a supreme source of help to all and cared for those from every walk of life.

If any man wer at dissese, He couthe thame wel comforth & plese When thai were seke he wald tham ese.	42. He knew well how to comfort those in distress and cheer them, and he would care for those who were sick.
If gestis come, smale or grete, Als som men did to hym oftsithe, Whils thai wer sittand at ther mete, Gude curtasy couthe he kythe, And thof that he wald litil ete, His countenaunce was glad & blithe.	43. When entertaining frequent guests of varying rank, he was expert at making them feel at ease (showing them courtesy) as they sat at table and, although he ate little himself, he always appeared happy and cheerful.
Swete mynstralcy when he myght gete, Deuoutely he wald itt lithe, For than to God chaunged his mode, And oft he gaf tham of his goode, For thi thai spake thereso tha yode.	44. When he could, he engaged minstrels who played beautifully and he would listen to them devotedly as they influenced his thoughts towards God. He was often generous to them as they reported on their travels.
Of diuerse sayntis I haue oft redde, He was ful like in his lifyng; With gastly fode for he hym fedde, Fastyng, wakyng, and prayng.	45. He was very like many saints of whom I have read in his way of life, for he fed on holy food, fasting and vigil and prayers.
With selke or hair if he wer cledde, He wald lat no man haue knawyng, All that him knew forthi hym dredde, Because of slike haly doyng.	46. He allowed no one to know how he dressed, whether he wore silk or a hair shirt. Therefore all who knew him respected him on account of such holy behaviour.
Als sone as euer the bel rang, To messe, or matyns, or euynsang, Wer he neuer so gret men emang, When he to God wald pray gastly.	47. No matter how important his visitors, he would immediately attend mass or matins or evensong as soon as he heard the bell ring.
Als he had ofttymes gret delite, He was be his one priuely, And oft vanysshed in his spirite.	48. Also he loved often to pray on his own and many times he was caught up in a trance.
He wald not shew him opynly, Ne for not like ane ypocrite, Yit myght nane perceyue certanly, How that he was ay soo perfite.	49. He made no open display of piety like a hypocrite, yet no one could tell for sure how he achieved such perfection.
Right wise he was and merciable Discrete in dome & not vengeable, Full of pite and resonable.	50. He was very wise and merciful, reasonable in judgement and not vengeful, full of pity and good sense.
Comonly when odir wer at rest, He went to contemplacion, Aftir matyns and no man wist. Withouten simulacioun, The verray crosse that is ful blist, He worshipt with deuocion, In mynde of him oft he it kist, Ihesu that therevppon was done.	51. It often happened that, after matins, unknown to anybody, while others were asleep, he devoted himself to contemplation. In true sincerity (without pretence) he worshipped the very blessed true cross and in his imagination kissed it, Jesus hanging there.

Appendix B

Sources and select bibliography

The names and abbreviations in the first column are those used throughout the text to identify authors and quotations.

Major sources of the life of St John

Ashby: *The Collected Works*, Durham, MS Cosin V.V.19 (c. 1530).
    Canon Thomas Ashby's summary of John's life with details of some of his miracles. He quotes material from Johannes Gielemans' life of St John in *Anecdota ex codicibus hagiographicis*. Gielemans (1427-1487) was a Bollandist living in Brussels. Translated in 2011 by Gerald Moxon.

Boniface: *Bonifacio IX, 1401, Anno 12, Lib 136*, Vatican Secret Archives; translated by Canon J.S. Purvis, 1924 (for details see below).

Capgrave: *Nova Legendae Angliae,* ed. Horstmann, 1901.
    John's life was added to Friar John Capgrave's collection in the 1516 edition. It is a rather verbose and rhetorical account. Translated in 2011 by Gerald Moxon.

Hugo: *Acta Sanctorum, 10th October;* Collecta, Digesta, V, Brussels, 1786.
    A most important source, written by 'Canon Hugo' in about 1390, probably a Bridlington canon himself. Translated in 2011 by Gerald Moxon.

Kirkstall: *The Short Chronicle of Kirkstall Abbey*, Thoresby Society, vol 42, pp. 54-55, 130n. (written around 1390).

ME Verse: *A Verse Life of John of Bridlington*, ed. Margaret Amassian, Neuphilologische Mitteilungen, LXXI, Helsinki, 1970, pp. 136-145. The manuscript is in Yale University Library (for details see below). An incomplete Middle English verse, probably written by a minstrel around the time of John's death in 1379. Translated in 2006 by Nicky Terry.

Other sources

AH	ed. Dreves, G.M.: *Analecta Hymnica Medii Aevi*, Leipzig 1905; vols. 28, 42, 43, 46.
BL	British Library.
Brid. Chart	Lancaster, W.T.: *Abstracts of the Charters and other Documents contained in the Chartulary of the Priory of Bridlington*, Leeds, 1912.
Dialogue	Anon, *The Bridlington Dialogue,* Mowbray, 1960.
CChR	Calendar of Charter Rolls (BL).
CPR	Calendar of Patent Rolls (BL).
CYS	Canterbury & York Society.
GC	Grosjean, P.: 'Collectanea, De S. Iohanne Bridlingtoniensi', *Analecta Bollandia* vol. LIII, 1935, pp.101-129.
LR 97	Lateran Regesta 97: '1400-1401', Calendar of Papal Registers Relating to Great Britain & Ireland, Volume 5: 1398-1404; 1904.
Prickett	Prickett, Marmaduke: *Bridlington Priory*, 1831/1835.
PRO	Public Records Office.
Purvis	Purvis, J.S.: *St John of Bridlington,* Journal of the Augustinian Society, Bridlington, no.2, 1924.
Purvis Office	Purvis, J.S.: *The Office of St John of Bridlington*, 1927.
RS	Rolls Series (BL).
TE	*Testamenta Eboracensia*, vols. I-VI, Surtees Society.
WA	Wollaton Antiphonal, MS250, Manuscripts & Special Collections, Nottingham University, Office of St John of Bridlington, folios 411-413.

WAC   Walsingham, Thomas: *The St Alban's Chronicle,* ed. Riley, RS.28.
WHA   Walsingham, Thomas: *Historia Anglicana,* ed. Riley, vols. I & II, RS.28.
WYN   Walsingham, Thomas: *Ypodigma Neustriae,* ed. Riley, RS.28.
QMS   Anonymous 3-part Mass *Quem Malignus Spiritu,* Early English Church Music Vol. 22, Fifteenth-Century Liturgical Music: II, ed. Margaret Bent, 1979, Stainer & Bell for the British Academy.

Bridlington Manuscript
Bayle Museum MS, *Breviarium Augustinense,* c.1380.

British Library Manuscripts
Add. 24062, fol 7v. licence to send money to Rome for John's canonisation.
Add. 35285. XIII cent. office book from Guisborough (Yorks.), fol. 167v. – added in later hand an imperfect office to St John of Bridlington. Fol. 170v. – Calendar for May, under 7 (nonnas) *Sancti ioannis episcopi beuerlaco*; fol. 172v. under October 10 in later hand added *Sancti Johannis Brilyngton d/uplex/ f/estum.* Under 25 October only Crispini 7 Crispinus.
Add. 50001. Former H. Yates Thompson Library MS 59. Hours of the Virgin, with Hours of the Cross. Sarum. So called 'Hours of Elizabeth the Queen', c.1420-30, probably London, most lavishly decorated. The original owner in not known. Later in XV cent. the volume passed to Cecile Neville (fol. 147), the wife of Henry Beauchamp and then later of John Tiptoft, Earl of Worcester. At the end of XV cent. it came into possession of Elizabeth, daughter of Edward IV and wife of Henry VII, hence its name. In a few blank pages at the end have been added, in hands of the XV cent., prayers and services for the Trinity, St Thomas of Canterbury, St Anthony and John, Prior of Bridlington. They may have been added by the Beauchamp/Neville couple, since the Earl of Warwick was so fond of the saintly Prior.
Add. 82946. Book of Hours, Sarum use, c1420. Contains calendar for Diocese of York, tables for Easter and astronomical tables; devotions on the Passion and Hours of the Virgin. Suffrages to many saints including Thomas Becket and John of Bridlington. Origin – England and Bruges.
Cot. Dom. A12, fol. 140r. Kirkstall Chronicle.
Cotton Vitellius E. Contains sketches of four Priory tombs, including those of Prior Gregory and Robert the Scribe. The one untitled sketch may be of St John's shrine.
Harley 955. Early XV cent., belonged to Syon Abbey; fol. 55v. – De *sancto Johanne de Beuerlaco* Antiphon; fol. 56r. De *sancto* Johanne Bridlingtonie Antiphon.
Royal 2A xviii / Rennes, Bibliotheque Municipale, MS. 22, c. 1400-10. Prayers, beautifully decorated, most probably by Flemish masters. Fol. 7v – a miniature of St John of Bridlington; ff. 8r-v – part of office of the above. Since the first part of the Royal MS was cut off from MS 22 and was pasted into its modern position, the original destination of the book is unclear. The second part of the Royal manuscript was probably executed for John de Beaufort, 1st Earl and Marquis of Somerset (1397, but deprived of the higher title in 1399, died 1410) and Margaret de Holand his wife, whom he married in or before 1399. The Rennes MS was owned by Richard, Duke of York, and his wife, Cecile Neville, parents of Edward IV. Noticeable is the Neville connection, as with Add. 50001.
Royal 17B, xliii, fol. 132r; an illustration to William Stranton's vision of St Patrick's Purgatory, probably of St John of Bridlington.
Sloane 2321, Hours of the Blessed Virgin Mary, a fine illuminated XV cent. book. The inclusion, in the lower border surrounding the miniature on fol. 41, of a coat of arms has led to this Book of Hours being linked to Sir Bertin Entwisle, a hero of Agincourt, after his marriage to Lucy, daughter of Sir John Ashton, in 1437; after her husband's death, she had her residence in Northampton. Fol. 141v. De *sancto iohanne de beuerle* antiphon; fol. 142r. De *Sancto* iohanne Bredelingtoni Antiphon.

Cambridge University Manuscripts
Fitzwilliam College, MS38. Augustinian breviary of Dutch origin: ff. 469-470, Office of St John.

Sidney Sussex College, MS33, D2.11. Missal, York Use (1460-80): Office of St John.

St John's College, MS129, xv. Hymn for St John of Bridlington (*Miles Christi gloriose*).

Oxford University Manuscripts
Bodleian Library
Digby 53, fol. 68v. About Henry IV and the translation of St John; also some hymns from Bridlington.

Douce 362. A calendar from c. 1400, probably of northern English origin. Entries for St John of Bridlington on May 11 and October 10.

Lat. Liturg. fol.2. A hymn for St John (*Salve sancte prior*).

Laud. Lat. 5. A psalter from the Austin Priory of Guisborough, late XIII cent. (see also BL. Add. 35285). At some point later it was owned by the Percy family, whose patron saint was St John of Beverley. Fol. 7v. Calendar for October: under October 10 added in later hand *Sancti Johannis Byrlyngton duplex festum*, under 25 only Crispini 7 Crispinus. In May there is no entry for either.

Laud. Lat. 114. Psalter, from Austin canonesses' abbey of Lacock (Wilts.), late XV cent., abundantly decorated. Fol. 5v. Calendar for October: under October 10 *Sancti Johannis de Bridlington iij Dignitatis* in the same hand; St John of Beverley is not mentioned. Neither of them is listed for May.

Rawl. C. 142, fol. 262. Office of St John of Bridlington.

Rawl. C. 466. A Calendar in a Statute book, XIV-XV cent. from northern England. Fol. 14r. Calendar for May: Johannis de Beuerlaco under May 7, added in later hand; *trans/latio/ Johannis de Bridlingtona* – under May 11, added in hand even later. Neither of them is mentioned in October.

Rawl. C. 939. An Ordinary of 1288 from the Austin canons' abbey of Osney (Oxon.). Fol. 5v. Calendar for October: under October 10 added in later hand *Sancti Johannis de Bridlingtona maius duplex*, under 25 only Crispini 7 Crispiniani. Nothing about either of them in May.

Corpus Christi College Library
MS. 192. A XIV cent. collection from the Austin priory of Llanthony Secunda, Gloucestershire containing a calendar with St John of Bridlington on October 10: *Sancti Johannis presbiteri et confessoris priors de Bridlyntona duplex festum lectiones IX*.

New York, Pierpont Morgan Library
MS. 105. Hours of the Virgin for Sarum Use, profusely illustrated, XV cent., 1420-25, Rouen, for Sir William Porter of Lincolnshire. Fol. 52, a detailed miniature of St John in Augustinian robes and hat. The previous folio has St John of Beverley.

Paris, Bibliothèque Nationale Manuscript
MS. Lat. 17993. A XIV cent. Franciscan Psalter of Italian provenance, preceded by a calendar having a XV cent. insertion on October 10: *S. Johannis de Brintheltona confessoris*.

Yale University Manuscript
Beinecke Collection, MSS 331. The Middle English Verse Life of St John is appended to a copy of *The Fire of Love* by English mystic Richard Rolle (1290-1349).

York Minster Library Manuscript
Add. 2, ff. 411-413. Bolton Hours: Office of St John.

Bibliography

Allmand, C.: *Henry V*, London, 1992.

Bowers, Roger: *Choral Institutions*, part 5. PhD thesis, University of East Anglia, 1975.

Burton, J.: *The Religious Orders in the East Riding of Yorkshire in the 12th Century*, EYLHS, 1989.

Cecily, Sr.: *St John of Bridlington*, Bridlington, 1979.

Curley, Michael J.: *John of Bridlington*, Oxford Dictionary of National Biography, 2004-5.

Dresvina, Juliana: *St John of Beverley, St John of Bridlington – Blurring a Border between Two Saints' Cults,* Oxford, 2003.

Earnshaw, J.R.: *A Reconstruction of Bridlington Priory*, Bridlington, 1975.

Easting, Robert, ed.: *St Patrick's Purgatory*, EETS, 298, 1991, pp. 77–117.

Harper, John: *The Forms and Orders of Western Liturgy*, Clarendon, 1991.

Heath, Sydney: *Pilgrim Life in the Middle Ages*, T. Fisher Unwin, London,1911.

Hughes, Jonathan: *Pastors and Visionaries – Religion and Secular Life in Late Medieval Yorkshire*, Woodbridge, 1988.

Ingram, E.I.: *The Manor of Bridlington and its Lords Feoffees*, Bridlington, 1977.

Jennings, Bernard: *Yorkshire Monasteries*, Smith Settle, 1999.

Knowles, David: *The Religious Orders in England*, Cambridge, vols. I-III, 1948-59.

Lamb, J.W.: *A Guide to Bridlington Priory Church*, 1970.

Lyte, C. Maxwell: *A History of Eton College, 1440-1875,* MacMillan, 1875.

Mortimore, M.J.A.: *Bridlington School - A History*, Alan Twiddle Publishing, 1999.

Neave, David: *Port, Resort and Market Town – A History of Bridlington*, Hull Academic Press, 2000.

Neave, David & Susan: *Bridlington, an introduction to its History and Buildings*, Smith Settle, 2000.

Parsons, Anna: *The Use of Guisborough*, Exeter University PhD thesis, July 2004.

Southern, R.W.: *Western Society and the Church in the Middle Ages*, Penguin, 1970.

Spencer, B.: *Pilgrim Souvenirs and Secular Badges*, Stationery Office, 1999.

Thompson, J.: *Historical Sketches of Bridlington*, 1821; Free Spirit Writers, 2007.

Twemlow, J.A.: *A Miscellany presented to John MacDonald Mackay*, Liverpool, July 1914, pp. 128-131.

Twemlow, J.A.: *The Liturgical Credentials of a Forgotten English Saint*, Menages, Paris, 1913.

Victoria County History: *Yorkshire North Riding; East Riding.*

Webb, Diana: *Pilgrimage in Medieval England,* Hambledon & London, 2000.

Weller, Philip: *Music for Henry V and the House of Lancaster*, Hyperion CD notes, 2011.

Wylie, J.H: *The Reign of Henry V*, 3 volumes, London, 1914-1929.

Appendix C

Last Wills and Testaments

From Heath, Sidney: *Pilgrim Life in the Middle Ages*, 1911, p. 32:

1400. Roger de Wandesford of Tireswell in Notts recalled specifically that he had promised to visit the 'glorious confessors' at Beverley and Bridlington when 'I was in serious danger of the waves of the sea and almost drowned between Ireland and Norway' (Test. Ebor. i (SS, 4), p. 187).

1404. Matilda, wife of John Holbeck, citizen and merchant of York, left a silver-gilt necklace, set with gems, to be hung on the tomb of St John of Bridlington.

1433. Benedict, minister of the church of St David's, said that Master Henry Wells and Dom John Sutton were to have £10 to go on his behalf to Bridlington, Beverley and Walsingham and was anxious that the money should be released to them 'so that they can fulfil my purpose with all possible speed after my death' (Register of Henry Chichele,ii, p. 485).

1466. Wm. Boston, of Newark, chaplain, buried before the altar of St Stephen in the parish church of Newark, ordered his tomb to be covered with a marble slab, on which should be placed a marble figure of his father, and another of himself. He also left 26s. viijd. for a priest to make a pilgrimage for him to Bridlington, Walsingham, Canterbury, and Hales.

1472. Wm. Ecop, Rector of the parish church of Heslerton, in the East Riding, ordered a pilgrim to visit the shrine of St John of Bridlington, and seventeen other holy places named, and for the pilgrim to pay fourpence at each holy place visited.

1485. Dame Margaret Pigot, daughter of Wm. Sywardby, Esq., of Sywardby, left 'my Table of Gold to St John of Bridlington'.

In several of these wills the soul of the testator is bequeathed "to our Lord Jesus, to our Lady Saint Mary, to Saint John of Bridlington, and to all the saints in heaven".

1521. Agnes Constable of Withernwick bequeathed garments to Our Lady at Beverley and Hull, beads to St John of Bridlington and a silver heart to 'St John's head'

(Test. Ebor. iv, p. 153; v (SS, 79), pp.137-38, 186).

From Purvis, J.S.: *St John of Bridlington*, p. 44:

'In some Yorkshire wills, St John's name is coupled in a remarkable manner with that of the Blessed Virgin Mary to whom the Priory is dedicated'. He gives three examples:

Peter de Mauley, 8th Lord of Mulgrave, by will proved 14th September, 1415, ordered his body to be buried in the Church of St John of Bridlington.

William Keling of Bridlington, by will proved 18th January, 1458, ordered his body to be buried in the monastery of St Mary and St John of Bridlington.

In a grant dated 20th July, 1538 (S.P. Hen. VIII) occurs "the late Prior of St John's, Brydlington".

Appendix D

Grants and Charters to Bridlington due to veneration for St John

From Purvis, J.S.: *St John of Bridlington*, 1924, p. 48-49.

1388   Richard II, 'out of regard for John de Thweng, late prior,' gives licence to crenellate the Priory buildings *(see Appendix F)*.

1390   The Pope grants relaxation of penance etc, to pilgrims and those who give alms to the fabric of Bridlington Priory.

1391   The Pope orders Bishop of Palestrina to enquire about the miracles of John de Thweng, 'for whose canonisation King Richard, Queen Anne, and many prelates and nobles of the realm have made repeated and instant petition'.

1392   Richard II extends the manorial rights of the Priory.

1401   Pope Boniface IX decrees Canonisation and Translation of John the Prior.

1403   King's Knight, Peter de Bucton, to whom is given the custody of the Church at Scarborough, ordered to pay 110 marks yearly to the Prior, 'for making a new shrine in honour of the body of St John de Thweyng, late Prior'.

1405   The Church of Scarborough entirely transferred to Bridlington Priory.

1407   Church confirmed tax-free.

1411   Lawsuit and 'discord' between the Priory and Peter de Bucton about 100 marks, the residue of the value of Scarborough Church due from de Buckton to the Priory.

1409   The Pope grants mitre, ring etc to Prior Thomas and his successors.

1413   Confirmation by Henry V regarding the Church of Scarborough, with relief from the expenses of coast defence, 'on account of the King's affection to St John'.

1414   Similar to the above: 'on account of the King's affection to St John, whose body lies buried in the Church of the Priory'.

1420   Henry V sends a special messenger 'to the sacrosanct places of devotion of Bridlington and Beverley'.

1421   Renewal of the grant of Scarborough Church, 'for the King's affection to the glorious Confessor St John', with exemption of the working of the Alien Priorities Act.

1442   Grants of Henry VI, re-affirming the grants of Scarborough Church, with all profits and freeing the Priory 'within which rests the body of St John, sometime Prior', of all tithes, aids and clerical subsidies due to the King (also 1445).

1448   Henry VI issues a charter granting the Priory permission to hold three fairs annually.

1450   'For the great affection and singular devotion that we have to the glorious Confessor St John of Brydlynton and to the monastery of our Blessed Lady St Marie there', Henry VI allows the Priory to be exempt from an Act of Parliament to raise money for the King's debts. The Priory have bound themselves to maintain 'xii quarasters and a maister to teach them both gramer and song'.

1461   Edward IV confirms the grant of Scarborough Church.

1468   Edward IV sets the Priory free from all dues to the King, 'on account of the special devotion of the King to the glorious Confessor St John, sometime Prior'.

Appendix E

Miracles attributed to Prior John de Thweng

Miracles (before death)	Canon Hugo	Capgrave	Thomas Ashby	Walsingham	Gielemans	Papal Bull	Kirkstall Chronicle
1 Loaves into stones				●			
2 John's holy fervour	●	●		●●			
3 Sailors	●	●	●	●		●	●
4 Water into wine	●						
5 Stone fell on John	●						
6 Burning house	●						
7 Heavy ladder	●						
8 Corn increased	●	●			●		
9 Barley increased	●	●			●		
10 Great Barn sheaves	●					●	●
11 Birth of two girls		●			●		
12 Deformed girl		●					
13 Woman with fever		●			●	●	
14 Daughter of servant					●		
15 Foretold time of death	●						

Miracles (after death)	Canon Hugo	Capgrave	Thomas Ashby	Walsingham	Gielemans	Papal Bull	Kirkstall Chronicle
1 Summary	●	●			●		●
2 Drowned men	●					●	
3 Priest with evil spirit	●						
4 Woman and a devil	●						
5 Poisoned drink	●						
6 Stabbed in stomach	●				● sword		
7 Carpenter fell and died	●		●				
8 Biretta healed man	●				●		
9 One killed another			●●				
10 Young man died			●				
11 A pilgrim healed			●				
12 Women in childbirth	●						

Appendix F

Other medieval documents

1445 certificate (now at Eton College) which accompanied St John's relics

Universis Christi fidelibus ad quos presentes litterae pervenerint salutem. Noverit universitas vestra quod vicesimo sexto die Junii Anno domini Millesimo 1445 nos Robertus prior monasterii beate marie de Bridlington et eiusdem loci conventus ob piam et synceram devocionem quas Christianissimus princeps dominus nostri Rex Henricus sextus habet et gerit penes beatissimum confessorem Johannem quondam priorem Monasterii predicti deliberavimus eidem Christianissimo principi per manus illustris et prepotentis domini ducis Warrewici reliquias predicti beatissimi confessoris, videlicet unam iuncturam unius digiti et unam iuncturam spine dorsi eiusdem. In cuius rei testimonium presentibus sigillum meum conventuale presentibus est appensum. Datae apud Bridlington in domo nostra Capitulari die et Anno supradicte.

Translation:

To all the faithful in Christ to whom these present letters shall be delivered greetings. Know all of you that on the 26 June 1445 we Robert prior of the monastery of Blessed Mary of Bridlington and the convent of the same place on account of the pious and sincere devotion which the most Christian prince our lord the King Henry VI has and shows towards the most blessed confessor John one-time prior of the aforesaid (monastery) have delivered to the same most Christian prince by the hands of the illustrious and powerful lord Duke of Warwick relics of the aforesaid most blessed confessor, namely a joint of one finger and a joint of the backbone of the same (John). In witness whereof my monastic seal has been affixed to the present (letters). Given at Bridlington in our chapter house on the aforesaid day and year.

(translated by Dr R. Lutton)

The Licence to Crenellate (1388)

Richard by the Grace of God, King of England and France and Lord of Ireland to all to whom these present letters shall come, greeting. Know you that of our special favour and out of regard for John de Thweng lately Prior of Bridlington in the County of York, deceased, we have granted and given licence for ourselves and our heirs as far as we are able, to our beloved in Christ the present Prior and Convent of the aforesaid place, that they themselves [may] securely enclose that Priory with walls and buildings of stone and lime and fortify and crenellate the said walls and buildings and they will be able to keep the fortifications and crenellations in like manner to them and their successors in perpetuity without interference or hindrance from us or our heirs, Justices, Escheators, sheriffs or other our bailiffs or ministers or our heirs whomsoever, in witness of which things we have made these our letters patent. Witness myself at Westminster the 17th day of May in the 11th year of our reign.

By the king, himself. Ravenser.

Ingram, M.E.: *The Manor of Bridlington and its Lords Feoffees*, 1977, p. 135.

Grants made to Bridlington Priory *(see Appendix D)*

These grants to Bridlington Priory were specifically exempted from the operation of the Act of Resumption of 1450; but subsequently it was discovered that this exemption was inoperable, because the grants had been made by charter, whereas the exemption from the Act of Resumption extended only to grants made by letters patent. Technically, therefore, the Priory had ceased to enjoy its privileges; in July 1452, therefore, since the Priory was continuing to keep its part of the bargain, and since the King did not wish these arrangements to become void, he promptly granted all these privileges back to the Priory again.

CChR 1427-1516, pp.95-7, 118-120; ed. J. Strachey, Rotuli Parliamentorum, vol.5, p.183 ff., esp. p.188.

Appendix G

A comparative date chart

John de Thweng/ Priors	Archbishop of York	Monarch	Papacy	Various
c.1320 John born		1307 Edward II 1327 Edward III	1305 Clement V 1316 John XXII	(Pope at Avignon)
1340-1 became a canon				
1362 elected prior				
1379 died	1374 Alexander Neville	1377 Richard II	1378 Urban VI	
	1388 Thomas Arundel		1389 Boniface IX	1388 Priory granted licence to crenellate 1391 Henry Bolingbroke visited the Priory
	1397 Robert Waldby 1398 Richard le Scrope	1399 Henry IV		
1401 canonised				1400-09 Welsh rebellion
1404 translated	1405 Scrope executed 1405 Thomas Langley		1404 Innocent VII	1408 Prince Henry visited Bridlington
			1406 Gregory XII	1409 Pope granted mitre to Prior Thomas
		1413 Henry V		1413 Margery Kempe visited Bridlington
				1415 Battle of Agincourt 1421 Henry V's pilgrimage to Bridlington
1421 Wm. Sleightholme died		1422 Henry VI		
Prior was Robert Willy. 1447 Choir school founded by Henry VI			1431 Eugene IV (an Augustinian)	1440 Eton College founded by Henry VI 1445 St John's relics sent to Henry VI for Eton
		1461 Edward IV		1468 Taxes on the Priory waived

Appendix H

Liturgical Resources / Hymns for St John

Title	Grosjean p. 108	AH vol,page,no	MSS & location	text
Alma mater ecclesia	35142	43, 193, 324	Wollaton Antiphonal BL Colon 28	Y
Ioannes sanctissime	28719	28, 302, 127	Bodl. Rawlinson C142	Y
Ioanni devota mente	38459		" " "	
Terris anhelans ad Deum	20385		Simon Gourdani	
Salve sancte prior	40728	46, 269, 231	Bodl. Latin Lit f.2	Y
Bridlingtone prior pie	35961 (text)	46, 269, 230	BL Royal 2A	Y
Miles Christi gloriose	(text)		St John's Camb, 129, xv	Y
Alme pastor ovium		42, 231, 255		Y
Decantemus in haec die Iohannis preconia			Wollaton Antiphonal	
Iohannis merita fideles populi			Wollaton Antiphonal	

AH = Analecta Hymnica (searched all volumes except 48, 52-55).
Grojean – see Appendix B, Sources & select bibliography.

The Office of St John

	Office date	MSS 1	MSS 2	Details
1	10 October	S.Sussex, Camb. MS33, D2.11	Bod. Oxf. Rawl. C142, f.262	Missal, York Use (1460-80) See Purvis
2	11 May	BL Royal 2A XVIII	Bod. Oxf. Rawl. C142, f.262	See Purvis
3	10 October	Wollaton Antiphonal ff. 411 – 413	Camb. U. Lib Add.MS.4500	QMS – First Responsory
4	10 October	Bolton Hours, YMLib, Add. 2, ff. 206-7		Part of an office
5	10 October	Fitzwilliam, Camb, MS38, ff.469-470		Augustinian breviary, Dutch origin
6		BL Add. MS. 35285		Guisborough Missal, imperfect office, similar to Fitzwilliam MS
	Antiphon & verse 'Pater amantissime'	BL Harley 955		Syon nunnery, Middlesex